Rising From the Ashes

My 20+ Years with Mental Illness

Stephanie Paige

You're Not Alone

Stephanie Paige

*Dedicated to my husband, daughter, parents,
and all those who struggle in silence*

TABLE OF CONTENTS

My First Time Was When I Was 14:
An Introduction

MY FIRST TIME was at age 14.

It sounds young, too young, but know when I say 'first time' I mean my first time dealing with depression.

This day and age, it seems as if everybody has been diagnosed or knows someone who has been diagnosed with this disease. A hurtful one... to those under its spell and those who are in the lives of those suffering. It has no cure. You can experience it at any time and each time seems to be different in some way.

I can list the symptoms of depression, but that can be easily found via the internet with Google or WebMD. Those symptoms are very common, but what it never mentions is what you feel at the core when you are under its spell. You will notice throughout my journey I will capitalize depression. You may ask yourself why? Aside from it being a name of a disease, I feel it deserves the capitalization for if you've ever suffered from it, you will know how much it takes from you both mentally, emotionally and physically.

My first time was at the age of 14.

My parents had just moved us from Brooklyn, NY, to a suburb of Connecticut for a better life. The city was changing. My parents did not feel safe having me play outside with my friends just like every summer before. They wanted the best for their kids. I may not have agreed, but after becoming a parent myself, I now understand. I was not a horrible child. Yes, I agree, more stressful than my older sister, but not as stress-causing as my brother.

I grew up in a typical household. I had a relatively normal childhood. We lived in a duplex in the part of Brooklyn, NY, named Canarsie. Within the three bedrooms, one and a half bath home resided my mother, my father, my older brother, my older sister and myself. I am the baby, four years younger than my sister, 10 years younger than my brother. I had birthday parties, enough food on the table, cable television, Atari, then Nintendo, and family dinners with my grandparents. There was nothing traumatic that would have caused my depression diagnosis except for a genetic link. I had a predisposition on my paternal side. I would not become aware of this until several years after my diagnosis.

By the time of the move, my brother was out of the house living on his own and my sister had already started college. I had just graduated from junior high school. Instead of joining my friends as they started high school in Brooklyn, my parents moved us to Connecticut. This angered me… immensely. Teenagers, for one, have their normal angst and now I had one more thing to be angry about. I was to leave the house I had known since birth, the neighborhood I grew up with and felt safe in, friends I had made from my elementary school days up through junior high. I had already been angry with them after being forced to go to the gifted junior high instead of my zoned school which left me, in my eyes, friendless at the time.

Looking back on it now it seems foolish. I made some awesome friends at that junior high school. That school also unlocked my creative writing abilities as that was the talent that got me into it. Now I was leaving. Still carrying the anger of the "junior high" thing, I now added the "moving" thing to it.

They made me a part of the move as much as they possibly could. Knowing my love of architecture, they brought me up to Connecticut to go house-hunting. That part I rather enjoyed. The houses seemed so big and I had so much fun 'picking' my room in each house. Of course, my word didn't hold weight on which house my parents would eventually choose, as I was not the buyer. I would get rather excited about getting a bigger room and a larger house. Although I was leaving my friends behind, I had one of my dearest friends with me; my dog, Nikki. Although a dog is not a human, we shared a special bond. Sometimes I thought she knew when I was sad; she would come to lay with me and lick my cheek. She was there to listen and at the time, a welcome friend who was not going to criticize me or blame me for something as I thought my parents did.

The move was made the summer of 1994. I would start my freshman year of high school that August. I remained in contact with several friends from junior high through snail mail and the telephone; communication before the age of the World Wide Web. This all helped me adjust until I started school. The beginning of that first year was a wakeup call to how nice and how cruel people could be.

When I first started, I was one of the new kids. Much of my school had grown up together. They all knew each other from as early as Kindergarten. There were three other new kids; we quickly became friends as we were the 'odd ones out.' I couldn't pinpoint why, but it always seemed as if the existing crowd felt threatened by us. We were all just trying to fit in somewhere with some people. The first two friends I made who were not 'newbies' I met in science class. These two girls seemed nice and even invited me to sit with them at their lunch table. However, I would soon find out that it was all a façade. The two girls had set me up to be humiliated; time has blocked out the memory, but not the vision of them with their cool friends, laughing at me during lunch.

That would be the first incident.

In those first few months, the newbies and I learned quickly that we had to stick together, and eventually we would befriend another outcast native to the school. We called ourselves The Five Musketeers. They were the nicest people, never hosting judgment about who I was or where I came from.

Meanwhile, the popular kids felt they needed to have more fun with us outcasts. Since I was from Brooklyn (or as they called it "the hood"), the popular kids had quite a fun time picking on me, the girl from the inner city. I was being harassed almost daily, people asking if I was part of a gang. They wanted to know what my gang colors were, who my posse was. At first, I was amused over these country bumpkins. I was never in a gang... heck, I didn't even know where the nearest one hung out when I lived in Brooklyn. The kids persisted for weeks. One day I finally cracked when they asked if I was in a gang and owned a gun that I shouted back, "Yes, and if you keep bothering me, I am going to shoot you."

This was a lie; I was never in a gang, I did not and have never owned a gun. But above all, I would never have actually hurt any of them.

This story is just an example that aided in the start of my depression. I was already becoming one pissed off teenaged girl. I was so angry about the happenings at my new school along with the move that I became a cranky ass at home. I complained about everything. I argued with my parents constantly. Asking, "Why did you have to move me up here?" was almost a nightly occurrence. I didn't come out and say, "Listen to me, I am calling out for help here," because I was one who thought I could handle anything (and to be frank, not much has changed). Those words were my first cry for help.

My first experience with therapy was about to occur.

I am not sure where my parents found out about the group therapy, but one day after school my mother drove me about 20 minutes away to a teen group therapy session. The first thing I remember is seeing several other kids like me staring at the floor or the wall with angered expressions on their face. My impression was, "What the heck is this? How are they going to help me?!" I am not sure how much talking any of us teens did that first day.

I attended every week for a few months. I noticed all of us came more alive every week. The discussions focused on the root to our frustrations. As a result of the treatment, I became more engaged with my friends at school and started being happy. I hadn't felt that since the move.

The therapists taught us to adjust our thinking, to see what triggered our anger. It was my first step in realizing I wasn't angry with my parents as much as the situation of moving to a new area with peers who grew up in a completely different type of lifestyle than I did. Was I mad with them or myself for not being able to cope better? I began to see high school as a four-year journey and in those four years, I could learn to ignore those that chose to annoy me because I was different. I learned that being weird was okay because that weirdness is why I had the great friends I did have in high school.

I wish I could say I was depression-free the rest of my years in high school, but I wasn't. A few months shy of graduation and the evil demon returned to haunt me...

Major Depressive Disorder (MDD) entered my life at 14 and hasn't left me since. There have been years I have been free of its grip, but most of the time MDD has controlled me.

This book follows the beginning of my blog to present day with more expanded pieces. After succumbing to my sixth episode of MDD three years ago, I decided I would express my thoughts and my feelings through writing. I wanted to let others know what it was like to experience this illness. Rising from the Ashes, the blog, was born in January 2015. I still blog there today. I welcome you to follow me through the ups and downs of living with both MDD and GAD (and my former Postpartum Depression, Postpartum Anxiety, and mild PTSD).

As for me, now I am doing well and learning to live contently with my current diagnosis: Persistent Depressive Disorder (PDD) with episodic MDD, and GAD.

Almost a Week Ago
January 21, 2015

...I WENT EIGHT YEARS back in time. I admitted myself to short-term psych at the hospital. This was not an easy decision, but now being out with a clear head, I know it was best for me.

This bout of depression and anxiety has crippled me. The amount of weight loss, the constant body ache from shaking, the irrational thoughts. If I'm being honest, it was just as bad as my PPD (Postpartum Depression). They're tied.

Last Wednesday, I had a manic-depressive episode in front of many people who I wished would never see me this way. I'm just happy that these people are my good friends and were there to help. Jimmy, my husband, drove me to the hospital where I was admitted overnight to the Behavioral Crisis Center. It is a terrifying place, but that is a story for another time.

In the morning, I had a psych consult with the same doctor who saw me eight years ago for my consult for PPD. This time, she saw no need to admit me. I was taken home.

At home, my anxiety rose. My house scared me. My bed scared me. Sleeping scared me because I thought I either wouldn't sleep or wouldn't wake up. I was delusional. As Jimmy brought our daughter to dance that evening, my parents brought me to my psychiatrist appointment. I told her I was afraid to be alone, afraid of what I might do to myself. She did not like the things I was saying and back to the hospital I went. This time I stayed; five days in short-term psych. This was the best decision I made. I was discharged yesterday.

I will go further in-depth at another time but for now, I would like to end with thanking the staff of 6/7 West, especially my nurses. I miss them a lot.

I Am a True Believer

January 27, 2015

...**IN EXERCISE** as an additional medicine for both anxiety and depression. I have many friends who agree and many who disagree. I think for those who disagree it is a matter of finding that one form of exercise that you absolutely LOVE.

It wasn't easy for me to find it. Let's go back in time... back to my bout of depression in 2008. My daughter had just turned two. I was having a stressful time at work, and once again I recognized my depression symptoms just a tad too late. My psychiatrist put me on Lexapro, the occasional Xanax, and Trazodone for sleep. The medication helped a great deal, but I still had this constant sad, mopey feeling.

Enter my therapist; he would constantly tell me to exercise. Exercise releases endorphins or feel-good chemicals. I heard him loud and clear, and even attempted some Nintendo Wii fitness. I just did not love it. I would schlep down to the basement to do 15 minutes, three times a week to feel mildly better. My therapist suggested hiking. Hmmm.... hiking... I did live right up the street from a city-owned park with many hiking trails. Could I really do this? One day in late fall I put on my sneakers and took a twirl around the white trail at the park. The white trail circles Parks Pond and is about a mile in length. At the end of the trail, I felt... refreshed! I felt rejuvenated! This was just what I needed! I finally found a form of exercise I enjoyed.

Then problems hit; winter in Connecticut. How does one hike in the deep snow?!

"Don't worry," my therapist said, "I have a solution for that, too… snowshoeing."

Snowshoeing?! Was he out of his mind?! I would fall over and look like an idiot. Isn't snowshoeing for older people?! Nonetheless, he persisted, encouraging me to try it. The cost is minimal (just the price of snowshoes and poles) and the learning curve is very quick. I was doubtful, but I did want to enjoy a sport in the winter that had me outside. Being outside made me happy. I ended up having my husband buy me snowshoes for Christmas that year. He spent all of $75 for the shoes, poles and a carrying bag. I opened the snowshoes on Christmas. I even tried them on…

…but it was a year before I actually took them outside.

The fear of looking foolish plagued my brain until the winter of 2009. We finally had a decent snowfall and after another year of talking with my therapist, I finally had enough confidence to strap the snowshoes on and go out. Wouldn't you know it; it was fantastic!!! I even enjoyed snowshoeing more than hiking!

There is a peacefulness with snowshoeing that isn't quite there when hiking. This tranquility lies in the fact that the world is silent when it snows; no one dares to venture outside. Under that sun that first time, producing a fresh trail with my snowshoes, was a rebirth. I made these footprints. I exist. That year I went out snowshoeing probably about 10 times (which was fantastic because the next two years did not produce enough snow).

Last year, my last snowshoe of the season was perfect and fell on my birthday. It was a great end to my day. I still yearned to strap on the snowshoes, but it was a nice way to say goodbye to the snowshoe season and hello to the spring hiking season.

With my depression back this year, I had a very hard time pushing myself to exercise. First off, I wasn't eating enough for me to burn calories. I was barely eating 1,000 calories a day. In addition, after six bouts with this disease, I fell victim once again to not enjoying what I used to. Once released from the hospital and on my antidepressant for a week and a half, I felt more and more like myself and because of that, exercise was on my brain. When six inches of snow was forecasted last Friday night into Saturday morning, I told myself I was going to snowshoe! Sunday, I strapped them on and took myself into the city park and walked my usual snowshoe path of the three hayfields; it was euphoric!

If you are suffering, and you've tried many forms of exercise that you just seem to trudge through, I suggest trying something new. In addition to hiking and snowshoeing, I love Zumba Fitness. So much so that I became an instructor last summer, although I'm not teaching anywhere now. I admit as a gym-goer, I hate doing cardio there. I slog through it. I'd much rather hike, but I go because I love to strength train with weights there. Maybe you've tried hiking and it wasn't your cup of tea. Perhaps for you, it will be yoga or CrossFit or running. Expand your horizons and challenge yourself, you may be surprised at the results it has on your mood.

When the Joy Fades

February 6, 2015

WHEN MY BEAUTIFUL baby girl was born, I felt euphoria from the second her shoulders emerged from me. I had never been so happy. To know this little baby was all mine; she was all I ever wanted since I was a child playing house with my dearest friend. I would constantly pretend my Cabbage Patch Kids were my babies. I always wanted to be a mother, and now I was one.

The pure glow continued as I was moved from labor and delivery into recovery. I saw elation on my husband's face as he got to push the lullaby button, marking the birth of our baby girl; the lullaby playing throughout the hospital, spreading a little joy. Little did I know how much that lullaby would mean to me.

I held her; my Sophia Faye, my wise fairy. She was so small, yet so beautiful. I treasured her cooing and even embraced her cries. I was on a high, wishing I would never come down. She stayed with me until bedtime, so I could attempt to get as much sleep as possible before returning home where my sleepless nights would begin. One night in the hospital, I awoke and started to panic. It had been five hours since she was brought to me for feeding. The worry was beginning. Where was my baby girl?! I made Jimmy go get her. The nurses didn't bring her because she was asleep and one thing you learn is to never wake a sleeping baby.

The day came to bring her home. This child I brought forth into the world. I couldn't believe it. People were entrusting her life to me?! I felt like a child myself and I was 26. Things seemed to be going well until Jimmy was called into work; so much for two weeks off. His boss claimed it was because our child arrived almost three weeks early. Out of the 10 days Jimmy should've been home with me, he was home for only four of them. Fortunately, my mother did come to help.

Feeding became another issue. My baby girl had no issues latching, but she just felt like it was sleepy time once she did. Okay, that was no problem, I would supplement with formula. After, I began to worry she wasn't gaining weight. I began to fret that she didn't cry enough. I worried she was too hot or too cold. With all this worry, I started to have issues sleeping. This should've been the first clue.

Two weeks after her birth, the baby blues I was experiencing grew into Postpartum Depression. Aside from lack of sleep, I was barely eating and whatever went in me was quickly thrown up. Crying was an event that occurred at least six times a day. Then the thoughts moved in.

"What have I done?!"

"Her crying makes me want to rip my hair out."

"They'd be better off without me."

"I'm useless."

"I hate her. I hate myself for hating her."

"I can't stand to be around her, I can't stand to

be around me."

"I wish I could turn back time."

"I'm going to run away!"

The last thought plagued my mind for the two weeks before entering myself in short-term psych for the first time. I planned my escape in detail; from when Jimmy would be at work to going to the bank to withdraw money. However, I always froze on where to go. I was torn. I didn't want to be alone, but I didn't want Jimmy or my parents to find out.

Exactly one month after my baby girl was born, I was brought to the emergency room by my mother. Jimmy left work to meet us there and my sister was watching Sophia. In the ER, I began to tremble like I never have before. The anxiety kicked in. Silly me wanted to come because I was worried I was malnourished due to constant vomiting. Once in the room, the only doctor brought to me was the psychiatrist. The same psychiatrist I just recently saw for a consult. She questioned me and felt I needed to be admitted. Her next question was, "Are you willing to admit yourself?"

I thought about this. I thought about what I was doing to Jimmy, my mother, my father, my sister, and Sophia. Reluctantly, I answered; yes.

This was the beginning to me getting better. This was day one of 12 days I would be there. Twelve days of therapy. Twelve days of playing with my medication. Twelve days of discovering things about myself. Twelve days to understand the postpartum depression that overtook me like an alien.

Admitting I Am Certifiably 'Crazy'
February 25, 2015

MY FIRST HOSPITAL hospitalization for my mental health started on November 16th, 2006, exactly one month after the birth of my daughter. Although I needed to admit myself to the short-term psych unit, it was extremely hard for me to conclude that I was being hospitalized in a psych ward. It was hard for me to realize that I was indeed, now certifiably crazy. I was amongst so many other people in for various reasons… depression, schizophrenia, anxiety, addiction. I thought of myself as the most 'normal' one there. After all, I was only 'crazy' because of the hormone drop from having a baby. I wasn't like these other people!

But, I was and still am.

While there, all of us patients had to attend various group therapies. We had morning meetings where we would pick inspirational quotes and make our goal for the day. We had art therapy. We had actual group therapy where we shared our stories and then we would wrap up at night to see if we achieved our goals.

The first day that I was there, I was still under the impression that I wasn't mentally ill, therefore, I did not join the group. By the second day, the nurses and therapists forced me downstairs. I went to the group but under protest, remaining exceptionally quiet. I listened to all the other people speak. Things still weren't clicking and linking up in my head.

Then, one day, an older gentleman spoke about his depression and how his wife and daughter had abandoned him in response to him not seeking help. Years that he could have gotten treatment... years that he could have had with his family... wasted. It wasn't until he described his symptoms that I realized I had experienced mental illness for a lot longer than just postpartum. Sure, the hormonal drop didn't help, but like him, I had experienced the anger, the verbal abuse, crying, sleep changes, food changes and ultimately, distancing myself.

He and I became good acquaintances while there in short-term psych. I pushed him to call his daughter and he pushed me to get better for mine, using his past as a cautionary tale.

I left 12 days after I admitted myself, into the loving arms of my husband, daughter, parents, sister, and in-laws. They were the only people outside of the hospital who knew of my diagnosis. I was embarrassed to be labeled mentally ill. I fed into the stigma. I didn't tell friends for a long time in the fear they would abandon me. After all, it took me days in the hospital to realize I was mentally ill and that I belonged there. How would others feel when the stigma on mental illness just grew more and more over the years?!

Eventually, I worked up the courage to share my story with my group; I was not abandoned but accepted. They wanted to help me. In fact, some were upset I never told them I was in the hospital, because they wanted to visit.

It was because of this overwhelming support that I became an advocate of dismissing false information about people with mental illness. I decided to tell anyone who would listen to my story. Not just my postpartum story… but my story since my first encounter with depression at 14. I may be medicated under the eyes of a psychiatrist and in therapy, labeled with mental illness, but I honestly am a relatively typical person. I may not appear to be mentally ill at first glance, but there's more to me than meets the eye. I am turning my experience into help for others, helping to tear down the walls of stigma.

Making Amends
March 9, 2015

LAST NIGHT I had a dream. I was diving deep into this dream when my alarm clock went off at seven this morning…

"…Wake up, don't sleep your life away…"

Normally, I gladly wake up, but today I didn't want to get out of bed. I didn't want to leave the dream. In the dream, I got to see T., my former foster son. I didn't want to leave him.

There was more to this dream than seeing T., which is why I call this the "making amends" dream. I was at T.'s daycare waiting for him to show up, to be dropped off by his new Daddy or Mommy (there's still a sting in my heart as I say that). It seemed as if I was an employee there. Every time the door opened, someone I wanted to apologize to walked through.

… Daycare Manager & Assistant Manager…

… Daycare workers in T's room…

…Birth to Three Workers (Birth to Three is a program that aids families with helping their infants and toddlers who experience developmental delays or disabilities)

… T.'s Social Worker…

During this dream I had deep conversations with the Birth to Three people, profusely apologizing that I screwed things up, I let them down. We went into how he was doing and how they would be leaving him soon, too, since he'll be turning three in a week.

Then I turned to my right and T.'s social worker was standing there. I once again apologized as I never got the chance to speak to him since before T. left. I was ashamed. I still am. I was in the middle of talking to him through tears when T. walked in. It was at that moment that I turned to look at him and smiled that my alarm clock went off...

"...Wake up, don't sleep your life away..."

This time I wanted to. I wanted to dive back into the dream. I wanted to hug him, to kiss him, to apologize to him. My cursed alarm clock stole that from me. It stole the most important thing, making amends with the adorable little boy I once called my son.

"...Wake up, don't sleep your life away..."

Thinking about it now, I wish I'd thrown that clock across the room out of anger of that stolen dream. Then again, the damn clock is right. There would be no good in sleeping my life away trying to enter that dream world again. I'd miss those around me now, those I love deeply, and hope to love me still.

Making amends... I know it is a part of many addiction 12-step programs, but I wonder if there should be a 12-step program for those who put their loved ones through hell due to depression and anxiety.

Step one... Breathe

Step two... Therapy

Step three... Medication

Step four... Meditation

Step five... Make amends

In my dream, all those people I apologized to

accepted and told me it wasn't my fault. I wasn't in control of my body and mind. I was sick. I still wonder though if these individuals would really accept my apology, including my former son.

"...Wake up, don't sleep your life away..."

I just wish this time I could have, just to hold T. once again. To hug him, give him one last kiss on his cheek and tell him, "I'm so sorry."

Triggers
April 1, 2015

WE ALL HAVE something in our lives that will cause us stress, tension, anxiety…

What happens when your biggest trigger is the people you love the most, your child(ren)? What happens when looking at them makes you want to vomit? What happens when even hearing them suffer from a cold makes you want to physically rip your hair out? What happens when hearing them whimper (not whine) makes you want to run from the house screaming?

This sounds horrible and cruel, yet this has happened to me twice in my lifetime. It is painful to admit, as I feel I'll be judged, and someone will call child services on me. No mother ever wants to think her child will drive her literally to insanity, but it happens. It happens more than people will admit.

The first time this occurred was almost nine years ago after the birth of my daughter. I felt alive when she was born. I treasured her. I watched her sleep. I gave her so many kisses and cuddles, and then one day it started to change. Her sweet innocent newborn face became ugly to me. The little noises escaping her once precious lips became like a crow's caw in sound. Her low cries for me to feed her or change her or even hold her became like a banshee screaming. All this happened in almost a blink of an eye.

I couldn't stand to be around her. I blamed her for what was happening to me. I began to hate her. I began to plan my escape, my freedom.

Am I an awful mother yet?

I felt that I was a horrible human being, let alone a bad mother for a few months. How could a mother hate her child?!

As if suffering from postpartum depression and anxiety once wasn't enough, it occurred again this past year with my foster son whom we were to adopt.

Once more, a little innocent child became my biggest trigger. Looking at him, thinking about all the responsibilities that came with him on top of the responsibilities with my daughter's generalized anxiety disorder, on top of work with very little help from my husband, and I broke down. His face with his cherub dimpled cheeks that I used to love to kiss caused me to dry heave into the toilet. His toddler gibberish that I found adorable now made me scratch at my arms with my nails. Worst of all, his coughing from his continuous colds made me want to rip my ears right off my head.

I don't blame my husband for the lack of help. In both instances, it was my alpha personality that prevented him from helping more. I thought I could do it all. It was more painful with my foster son because I was in such a good place mentally, emotionally and physically. I really thought I could do it all again.

Triggers; some professionals say that they cause the stress and the tension, but in my case, the stress and the tension caused my daughter and my foster son to become triggers. Looking at them caused severe anxiety and ultimately depression. It's hard living with that. It's hard to admit that at two points in my life, I was a horrible mother, an incompetent mother.

I will always carry guilt over that. Even as I stare at my daughter now with awe that this beautiful girl is mine… even as she laughs, and I smile… even as I once again continuously hug and kiss her…

I feel the guilt that at one point, just looking at her gave me such negative feelings.

My Biggest Fear
April 29, 2015

I HAVE SUFFERED from this horrible mental illness, depression, for most of my life. Twenty-one years out of the 35 years I have been on Earth. That's a lot. Thinking about it drains me. Thinking about each battle, reliving it in my head even for a few seconds exhausts me on all planes; physically, mentally, and emotionally. As I age and suffer, it takes more energy out of me than the last time. I survive, stronger in ways, weaker in others.

This last time nearly killed me. No, there was no suicide attempt, but sheer exhaustion from the anxiety. The new symptom of panic attacks and anorexia had basically developed, and it utterly scares me. I'm scared if I suffer a seventh episode of major depressive disorder (MDD) it will indeed end me, and I'll leave my child motherless and my husband a widower. It seems as if my symptoms are progressively getting worse with each spell.

This past January, as I lay in the stark-naked room of the Behavioral Crisis Center, I had one of the scariest intrusive thoughts of my life. Facing what I felt was an infinite mental pain, I stared at a screw on the lunch tray table. Emaciated, weak, I thought about what I would do if I could loosen the screw. I wanted to give myself a lobotomy with it, push it in and keep twisting. Eyes flashing all over the room looking for something to act as a screwdriver...

I'm petrified. "What ifs?" run through my mind. What if I succumb to MDD's ugliness for the seventh time? How bad will I be then? What if there is a screwdriver within reach? What if it is worse and I succeed at slitting my wrist, unlike when I was 18?

In a normal state of consciousness, I would never even consider it, but when I'm suffering, deep into the depths of the ocean of depression, I am not sane. I am not me. I don't think about how my absence would hurt my child, my husband, my family. All I can focus on is how to rid my brain of rapid continuous thoughts, to rid my brain of thinking entirely, because if I am not thinking, I'll be okay. At least this is what depressed me believes.

To avoid a seventh time, I have agreed with my primary care physician, my psychiatrist and those at the hospital to remain on my antidepressant indefinitely. Of course, as a worrier by nature, I am horrified at what I may do if it fails me. If depression and anxiety take up residence once again... What I may do since it becomes more powerful, and exhausting each time...

Behavioral Crisis Center: Day 1
May 25, 2015

I WAS THEN taken not to the ER area like last time, but beyond it to an area I knew nothing about... The Behavioral Crisis Center. The sign above the monitored doors was metallic and nice looking, but they hid the blank depressive state that lied beyond the doors. Buzzed in, Jimmy and I followed the nurse.

I was then shown to a room. The walls were neutral with no decorative trim. The only object in the room was a twin-size bed centered on the floor. The bed had a slight illusion of hovering, the mattress topped with blue vinyl. No headboard, no footboard. The only decor to the bed was metal hooks for the sole purpose of strapping you down. No sheets or pillows were provided to me.

The security guard left his bullet-proof glass cube and entered my room. He dropped a plastic bag on my bed. A nurse followed with a stark white with blue design hospital gown and blue pants, size XL. The guard then proceeded to tell me to go into the bathroom and change, putting all my clothes and belongings in the bag.

I entered the bathroom and was somewhat shocked at what I saw. For one, the guard stood outside the door, there were no locks. The second thing I noticed was the lack of glass mirror so those like myself would not break it and harm ourselves. The mirror was made of metal and you would need a strong Phillips-head screwdriver to attempt to take it off the wall. I guess I should be happy there was still a toilet and not just a hole in the floor. In one corner was a shower stall with no curtain. I don't know why they couldn't add color. A burst of orange here, a splash of green there. Instead, I was faced with just beige and plenty of it. In fact, the only color I noticed was the blue vinyl that adorned the beds.

After I changed, I knocked on the door and the guard opened it, took the bag and made sure I went back to my room where Jimmy was sitting. I was unsure of what was going to come next. The bed still bare, I laid down and attempted to rest as anxiety still riddled my body. I started to shiver, not from nerves, but from the cold temperature of the room. When the nurse came back, she informed me that I would be talking with a psychiatrist and a social worker that evening to see what exactly they would do with me. I felt as if I were in limbo. I kept praying that they would come soon. I was desperate for help, hopeless, worthless, empty.

I asked the nurse if I could have a blanket. My teeth were chattering. She smiled and replied "yes" and that she would bring me two. She returned with the blankets and asked if I was hungry. I nodded and replied, "A little." She said she would return with a tray of food and to eat as much as I could, which in the end didn't amount to much.

As I lay there, Jimmy and I listened to the other patients. The woman next to me kept getting yelled at by the guard because she was leaving her room. She whined incessantly to use the phone to call her young son as he was going to bed soon. Over and over, "Please, please let me use the phone. I promise I'll be quick." The guard told her no, the phone was off use to patients unless it was for setting up plans for picking up. Within the next five minutes she left her room, the guard yelled, and she pleaded once again for the phone. This cycle repeated over and over almost the whole night.

My room was directly across from the locked doors, so I could witness everyone who came and went. The next arrival was a woman who was clearly drunk. She arrived on a gurney with several policemen and two EMTs. Nonsense was spewing out of her mouth. Her arms were flailing as she tried to hit the cops. Tired, I could barely lift my head to watch. I heard them move her into a room two doors down from mine with the bathroom in between. Still yelling, they stripped her and put her in the hospital uniform of the gown. I only know this because this same woman returned the next night after I came back, and I saw. It took the security guard, the two EMTs and the two cops to hold her down and change her. She was still screaming after they left.

Finally, the social worker entered my room. A nice middle-aged woman with medium length chestnut hair. She started asking me basic questions that I already told the ER triage nurse. My name, address, employment... Then came the tougher questions. Why was I here? Did I hear voices? Did I want to hurt myself, kill myself? What caused all of this?

I answered her honestly. At this point, I had no plans of hurting myself or attempting suicide. I told her I didn't deserve to be alive, and that I certainly didn't deserve to be a wife or mother. I told her I was an evil person for giving back my foster son. My husband and daughter could do far better than me and I expressed to her how much I wanted my husband to take our daughter and leave me. At this point, I cried about how worthless I was. She told me she was going to talk to my husband in another room and they left.

Laying there still shivering out of fear and being cold, I scanned the room. Banal, boring, empty, just like myself. The sounds of both my immediate neighbors still echoed frequently. I didn't belong here. I wasn't an addict like them. I didn't drown my sorrows with multiple glasses of wine or by shooting up some drug with a needle in my arm. Why couldn't they just bring me upstairs to the short-term psych ward? They would know how to help me. They had helped me before.

The social worker returned with Jimmy. She told me, honestly, she would send me home as she did not fear I would hurt myself or another person. What skewed her decision was Jimmy telling her about how delusional I was. With this, it was decided I would remain in the Behavioral Crisis Center overnight. I asked about seeing the psychiatrist that evening. She told me that they had left for the night and would see me the next morning. I became scared about staying the night in this place, but was so drained from all my anxiety that I didn't show my fear. Nor did I say anything. At this point, Jimmy was asked to leave.

"Give Sophia a hug and kiss for me. Don't make her go to school tomorrow. She's probably anxious and still awake."

"Okay, will do." And with that, he kissed me and left. This was around 11 in the evening.

The nurse came back with an anti-anxiety medication, a sleep medication, and a nasal decongestant spray. I swallowed the pills happily. All I wanted to do was fall asleep and escape this horrible place I was in. I received one more blanket that I needed on my body, but still lacked a pillow and had to use it for that purpose. I turned my body over as they shut the lights from the glass enclosure and attempted to fall asleep. Although I succeeded in some sleep, I woke several times to the screams of other patients and mostly to the sounds of vomiting. Their bodies were going through detox of alcohol or whatever their drug of choice was. At other points during the evening, I awoke because I was uncomfortable with no pillow and still freezing. I cried several times. Was this the new short-term psych unit? If so, I would rather suffer at home and risk getting worse. I began to question my decision to be there repeatedly. Good cop, bad cop. I know I needed to be there to see the psychiatrist because they would admit me, but this was such an awful place. Sounds of retching in the background only produced more fear and tears in me. I wanted to go home.

Due to my lack of sleep, no one needed to wake

me in the morning. At some point, maybe seven, the nurse came in as the security guard flipped on the lights from his glass cube. She took my blood pressure, temperature, and pulse. She asked me how I slept, how I felt. Shitty. I felt like complete and total shit. I told her I was exhausted, and my body felt terribly weak. I expressed my lack of sleep to her. She questioned if I would like some breakfast. I replied with a mumbled, "Okay, I'll try to eat it."

Breakfast was brought to me and it looked pretty good; pancakes with butter and syrup, scrambled eggs, cereal, and some fruit. I managed to eat one pancake and the fruit, and I was full. I continued to read one of the magazines from the hall when the psychiatrist finally came to my room. I almost vomited at the sight of her. Who should be the doctor to analyze me... the psychiatrist who asked me eight years ago, "Would you like to admit yourself?" Eyes already welling up at recognizing her, I just exploded and started to rock and cry. Why did it have to be her? The sight of her brought back images of my postpartum suffering on top of what I was experiencing currently. Déjà vu. I was asked the same questions asked by the social worker the night before. Instead of asking me whether I would like to admit myself, this doctor, the one I saw eight years ago, told me I could go home. She said I didn't belong upstairs at this time. I continued to cry. I repeated, "But I need help. I can't do this at home. I can't be alone."

I was handed a phone by the security guard to call someone to come pick me up.

Home? I couldn't go home! Home scared me. My room, once my calming quiet place, was now the scene of my anxieties. My bed was now a cause of nausea, not comfort. She wanted me to go home?! I hesitantly dialed the house number and my husband picked up.

"What's happening?" he asked.

"You need to pick me up," I said softly. "The doctor said I don't belong here."

There was a silence before I heard my husband respond, "Okay, but what about Sophia?"

"You'll have to bring her." I hung up.

The guard came back in with my bag of belongings. He asked what happened and I told him my husband was coming to get me with my eight-year-old daughter. I was told after I changed, I would be brought out to the ER waiting room to wait for them as the Behavioral Crisis Center was no place for a child. The guard then led me back to the unlockable bathroom to change back into my human clothes. After all that I experienced in the hospital that night, I cannot call my oversized gown and pants "human." Then again, I still felt more like a zombie. Pulling out my clothes, I quickly changed. Then I glanced at myself in the metallic mirror. What the hell was I going to do? The hospital was supposed to be my answer. Now I was never going to get better.

After I was done, I knocked on the bathroom door to be let out. Holding my box of cereal from breakfast, the guard led me through the ER that was already quite busy at nine am into the waiting room.

He explained to security that someone was coming for me and then he left. I felt alone even though there were a handful of people there. I folded my arms over my waist, pulling my coat closed as I was still cold. Then I waited, peering out of the multiple story window wall. As I usually do, I started to eavesdrop on a conversation between a nurse and an orthopedic patient waiting for her ride in a wheelchair. Normally, I find these stories fascinating, but I couldn't this time. The nurse's migration from South Carolina to Connecticut was enthralling enough for this overly depressed person. After about 20 minutes, I caught sight of my husband and daughter. Sophia ran through the doors and wrapped her arms around me.

"Mommy, are you all better now?"

My eyes filled with tears. I didn't want to tell her the truth. The only word to escape my mouth was "no."

I was not okay. I had no idea what was going to happen to me. The routine I had prior wasn't working. I became increasingly more mentally ill each day. It seemed as if every morning I woke up and a new body part hurt, or a new symptom emerged. The medication still had several weeks before it would even start working and that was if I was on the correct medication. Unlocking my daughter's arms from around my decreasing waist, I grabbed her hand and kissed it. I missed her, and I desperately hated myself for what I was putting her through since she was old enough now to know... to know that her Mommy was sick.

Should I Have Become a Mother?
June 30, 2015

MY GREATEST GIFT in this world is my daughter. She exudes so much love, and yes, quite a bit of whininess, but she is a wise and kind being. And... I probably never should have had her. I look back on my life and see the pain, the craziness, the hurt that my brain has caused myself and my family, and I wonder if I should have ever become a parent in the first place. When recanting my life's tale, my worst episodes of depression and anxiety surround my children... first with my daughter, and then with my former foster son. It is a formidable sign that my body is telling me all these years later: "Knock, knock, it is your brain calling..."

I listen now, but where would I be if I had listened at my third reoccurrence of depression in college as a 20-year-old? Would I even be married? Would my husband have left me then if I said a big NO to having children? I know, it is all a game of "What ifs." It isn't as if I could turn back time.

There are many people in this world to whom parenting seems almost easy when I look at them. They never fell victim to postpartum depression, anxiety... They never wished they could leave their spouse and child. They never thought about how horrible they were. Sure, there were tears during diaper changes, moments they wanted to scream, but these women went on to have more children. For me, each child had one cause and effect outcome on me: cause, anxiety. The effect, major depression. Not a normal outcome by any means, but one that I sit and think about often.

I should have never become a parent...

How can I say this when I have this beautiful little girl in my life? How she understands her mother's illnesses and can still love me, how could I say I should not have had her?

If I had known what would happen to me after her birth or after having my former foster son in the house, back then, would I still have desired so much to become pregnant?

My daughter is a gift I should not have been given. Therefore, I call her my greatest, most precious gift. She's my most delicate gift. She's amazingly perfect to me. Even with some of her minor difficulties, her anxiety, her whininess, her emotions, she is perfect. After watching her mother almost wither away, she didn't get angry with me for losing her "little brother." Instead, she was overly worried about losing me. She doesn't want to lose her Mommy. I am sure what she witnessed from me was extremely scary for her and with her anxiety diagnosis, I am sure she is more worried than she should ever be. It is not her responsibility to take care of me and I have expressed that to her.

My greatest gift, and to think here I am wondering if my life should have been without her? Please note my past tense in verbiage. Am I a bad mother for saying that?

Put yourself in my shoes for a moment so maybe you can understand. Now bend down and pretend you are tying the laces of my hiking boots. Let's travel back in time, almost nine years ago. You have just given birth to a beautiful and healthy baby girl. Life seems blissful. You cuddle your baby in your arms, giving her kisses at every opportunity. You think, *This is why I carried you for almost nine months, this is why I became a mother… to give and receive unconditional love.* Now picture you are home with this infant and within the first week of her birth, you become worried… overly worried. Is she eating enough? Is she sleeping too much? This quickly intensifies to a point at which *you* are not eating or sleeping. You are just existing as a shell of your former self and this shell is growing hatred toward this babe you so desired, and toward yourself. Think about wanting to run away because living seems unbearable. Now envision yourself saying these words, "Yes, I would like to admit myself into the short-term psych ward," one month after your baby was born. Imagine the guilt you have for missing 12 days of her short life at the time.

Would you even think about mothering another child?

I did. It wasn't until many, many years later that I even considered adopting or getting pregnant, realistically. Adoption was always a thought swirling around in my head since Sophia was three and my husband was extremely against me giving birth again because he couldn't relive the postpartum mental illnesses I had. So now, here I am, feeling the strongest I ever felt emotionally, mentally and physically. I am off medication, once again, for the last four years. Nothing can break me. I am invincible. Then, imagine getting that phone call after going through adoption classes and extreme amounts of paperwork, where someone tells you your family has been chosen. Think about a wide grin with happy tears escaping your eyes. You are living euphoria again. You are finally going to mother another child. You are going to provide them with a loving home. The happiness just boils inside of you. Imagine meeting this little boy you have been chosen for and looking into his eyes, realizing he looks more like you than your biological child. Picture instantly falling in love with him, yearning for the weekends when you, your husband and your daughter would go pick him up and get to play with him. Weeks pass and you start to get anxious about him moving in, about becoming a family unit of four, what you've always dreamt about.

Now, think of everything that comes with being a new full-time employee, wife, mother to a young daughter and now adding mother to a toddler with challenges into the mix. Your perfect vision is slowly cracking as you lapse into extreme anxiety and worry as this little boy will not eat or drink. Then you get the phone call from the daycare telling you they are kicking him out, claiming he is too much work because he doesn't eat or nap like the other kids. Growing tired and weary, you decide only you can solve this situation and find another daycare where they will "try" him out. The worry continues... will they kick him out, too? At this point, you have daily conversations at work with Birth to Three, and imagine during one of these days that you receive a phone call from your daughter's school nurse at the same time concerning a couple of recent anxiety outbursts. You now can't think because your mind is being pulled in so many directions and you have no idea where to start and like the alpha that you are, you still haven't asked for help. Think about when this once sheltered toddler is being sent home because he is sick. It has been so long, you have forgotten what it is like to have a sick toddler. You are now not sleeping because you wake at the sound of him coughing, which is often. Since you are not sleeping, you have become angry and more anxious and now, you too, are nauseous to eat. Within a few days of worrying who would stay home with him because you had no days since you are new to your job, you start to experience heavy breathing, heart palpitations, dizziness, an explosion of tears... your first real panic attack. Your dream of a family of four is now ruined as you fall victim to anxiety and a major depressive episode, once again leading you into the arms of the hospital's short-term psych ward. Imagine the shame you have for yourself, telling yourself it is all your fault you don't have your son anymore, you don't have your dream anymore.

Would you think about mothering another child?

This time, at the age of 35 and entering remission yet again for the sixth time for depression, my answer is a resounding… NO. All that I told you to imagine, I lived. Reliving it has some painful consequences. One of those consequences is my recurring thought of, "Should I ever have been a mother in the first place?"

*Previously Published in *Stigma Fighters Anthology, Vol. 2*

Mommy is Not going to Kill Herself
July 7, 2015

RECENTLY, MY YOUNG DAUGHTER, Sophia, has forced me to listen to a popular local radio station. Normally, I enjoy what I call classic rock (or '80s rock, which makes me feel old now that it's called 'classic'). I gave in to her request being that her recital songs play on this station and I, wanting to be a cool mom, decided to learn today's music. Honestly, with what comes next, it wouldn't have mattered what radio station was on.

On our day off, Presidents' Day, my eight-year-old daughter and I had a day of fun. This day included the most fun activity of all… visiting my psychiatrist. Note sarcasm. Because of this, I had to go to CVS Pharmacy to pick up my monthly medications. Sophia was with me. While we waited for them to be filled, Sophia was perusing the magazines… Then she asked… "What's going on with Bobbi Kristina (Whitney Houston and Bobby Brown's daughter)?"

Tough one. How do I explain this, mental illness, anxiety, depression and ultimately suicide to a young girl who suffers from anxiety herself and tends to turn everything into a catastrophe?! I thought about this for a minute.

I received some slack about talking to Sophia about this, but being that she can read, suffers herself, and has just witnessed her mother's sixth breakdown with a major depressive episode and anxiety, I felt I had to tell her something.

I told Sophia that Bobbi Kristina suffers from depression like Mommy does. I then explained that some people who suffer from depression feel that the only way to escape their pain and sadness is by taking their own life. I quickly followed that with…"Don't worry, Mommy is not going to kill herself. I've never ever had those thoughts. I've only had thoughts of running away. I NEVER had thoughts of killing myself."

I still find it unfathomable that I had to explain suicide to my child. I had no idea what would follow as Sophia's anxiety attacks can be triggered by almost anything and forces her to freak out at a moment's notice. Then she asked about herself. I told her for Mommy, anxiety is a major cause of my depression, but I'm an adult. I told her I know what to look for in her and right now, anxiety is her only issue.

Luckily, my explanation was enough for her and no anxiety attack followed.

Well, Sophia is a big thinker. She constantly thinks about everything. In the car the following morning, listening to her radio station, the DJ started to list off some news items starting with Bobbi Kristina and how she was still on life support but getting worse and her organs were beginning to fail. Sophia perked up and once again asked about her.

I explained that Bobbi Kristina must have been really depressed and tried to take her own life, but she didn't succeed. She then asked if she was okay. I told her that although she is still alive, she did a lot of damage to her body and most likely she will die soon.

Sophia then asked, "Mommy, are you going to do that?"

"No sweetie. Mommy is not going to kill herself."

She then told me how she was going to talk with her therapist about this at the next appointment and added that maybe she shouldn't listen to this radio station.

All this has left me in awe of her. At eight, she's picked up news by reading magazine covers and by little snippets on the radio. I can't hide everything from her. Most of me wanted to brush off the topic and lie to her, telling her Bobbi would be okay, but I just couldn't. This little girl has seen me shaking, crying, dry heaving, delusional. She's seen me at my worst and is old enough to remember and know that Mommy is sick. This innocent girl suffers herself with anxiety which makes her nauseous and delusional. I had to tell her something.

Mental illness is real. It effects all ages. It plays with your mind. It plays with your body. Unfortunately, it can occur in children. Unfortunately, children can witness their parents. My child both suffers and has witnessed her mother's suffering. I chose to explain it to her in a way a child would understand. I chose to break the stigma.

*Previously Published in *Stigma Fighters Anthology, Vol. 2*

It's Not Your Fault, Baby Girl; it's Nobody's Fault
July 23, 2015

YESTERDAY WHEN I arrived home from my much-needed self-care Zumba Fitness class, I noticed a folded-up piece of loose-leaf paper obviously torn out from a spiral notebook sitting on my bed. I have come home to these love-filled Sophia notes for years now. They always put a huge smile on my face. It's as if she is psychic and knows exactly when Mommy could use a little more love. But, this note was quite different and instead of a huge smile on my face, my eyes shed tears and it left me upset... at myself, once again. Sophia's note:

"Dear Mommy,

Your Depretion (Depression) was made from me because I didn't laugh when you rocked me. I didn't laugh when you cuddeled (cuddled) with me when I was a baby. I read the holl (whole) book thing that you wrote when you were in the Hopital (Hospital). I cryed (cried) because it said that.

I SO SORRY

love, Sophia

P.S. I miss T."

My initial reaction involved dropping the paper on the bed and running to her, my precious child, with arms open repeating, "It is not your fault, Sophia, it is not your fault." We embraced for several moments with her echoing, "Yes, it is. I didn't laugh enough as a baby; that made you sad."

This letter she read from me was written during my fifth episode of MDD, this time a bit more moderate instead of the two major episodes that straddled this time. At this time, Sophia had just turned two, a happy peppy toddler enjoying life. She had no clue that Mommy spent nights after work crying in her room as she slept peacefully upstairs. I never showed her my emotions because at this age she wouldn't grasp any concept of why her Mommy was crying multiple times a day. She wouldn't understand why her Mommy wanted to stay in bed. This time that depression inhabited my body had nothing to do with her, nothing to do with raising a toddler and its demands. This time it had to do with work and the huge amount of stress I was under there.

I had decided to write to Sophia during this time to explain to her why Mommy has her moments and what she is thinking and feeling during these times. I did this because I had no idea how many more times I would find myself locked up in depression's cell during her lifetime. The strange thing with the above letter from her is I don't recall saying I became sad because she didn't laugh enough. Whether or not I came out and literally said it or if she interpreted it that way, it hurt her.

I hurt my daughter, my main source of love and happiness in my life. That was enough reason enough to cry and hate myself.

How to explain this to her... how do I explain that my serial dealings of depression and anxiety are NO ONE'S fault when I don't believe it myself?! Therefore, I am still in therapy to this day. Yes, I didn't choose to become mentally ill, but I am the one who suffered from it. I am the one who put my husband and my parents through hell. I am the one reason T. is not in our house. I am the one who scared my daughter this past winter. I am the one who hurt my daughter in this letter. I am the crazy one.

Call it major guilt, shame, blame, regret... I have fleeting moments when it is all I can focus on and last night after reading this emotional letter from my almost nine-year-old daughter, I had one of these moments that has carried into this morning. I didn't know what to say to convince her it is not her fault. I explained to her Mommy is the one who is ill. She asked why depression made me feel those feelings I had written. I said it is just the way my brain is made up. She asked if it wasn't my fault, was it Grandpa's because I got it from him? I said no, it is the illness' fault...

The illness' fault... how do you blame something you can't see? Huh... very much like proving you are in fact mentally ill when there is no physical evidence... And then, how do you convince your child to blame this something you can't see when you feel like a hypocrite because you yourself can't do it?

Full of emotions, I sat on her bed later that night and told her that I loved her. I told her that I was sorry if it seemed to her like I blamed her. I was sorry that I scared her, I never meant for her to see me at my worst. I hugged her, kissed her, tucked her hair behind her ear and stared at this remarkably beautiful child. I explained how I missed T., too. I grabbed her hands and kissed them, and I told her (and myself) convincingly, "It's not your fault baby girl, it's nobody's fault."

Why Me? A Blessing in Disguise
July 31, 2015

I NEVER ASKED to be ill. I'm sure no one jumps up and down begging, "Pick me, I want cancer!" I don't see anyone paying to contract AIDS. I also can't picture anyone smiling when told they have multiple sclerosis. Believe me, I was not crying tears of joy at getting my mental illness diagnosis, especially in my early teens.

Twenty-one years later, I am still questioning, "Why me?" I had all these future plans that have since crumbled like an avalanche because of my depression label. Normal life events are tremendously stressful on me, not only mentally but physically. As far back as when my depression started, I can pinpoint the typical everyday life event that caused it:

At 14... we moved from my birth home to another state where I started high school knowing no one.

At 18... I felt neglected and unimportant as my adulthood birthday was almost ignored as my mother had to take care of my grandmother. (I do not blame my mother at all for this now.)

At 20... I had stressful classes at college.

At 26... I gave birth to my daughter.

At 28... I had climaxed at my job and was dealing with demanding responsibilities as the sole employee and the fact that I had nowhere else to go.

And, at 34... I was given another child through

fostering who was to become our son, but sadly, he had to be removed because of me falling into depression's arms again.

So, why me? Why was I given this present? Why every few years do I feel nothing? Why do I become apathetic, hopeless, helpless? Why do I become exhausted, achy, teary and anxious?

This gift, depression, is genetically linked on my paternal side, seeing more faces than I care to list. Over and over, I have asked whatever higher being is up there, "Why me? Why am I the 'lucky' one?"

Over the last 20 years of struggling, including a plethora of appointments with psychiatrists and therapists, multiple medication changes and research, I have gained much knowledge on the topic of depression. I have gained insight on how it affects me and what works for me regarding my recovery. And now, although I still sometimes ask, "Why me?" I have started to wonder if this illness is really a blessing in disguise. Is my depression a gift?

Recently at the conference I went to, I learned that thriving mothers, or thriving people in general, invite their anxiety in for tea. They embrace their anxiety. I have decided to apply the same principle to my depression. I am letting my depression join me for coffee and cake. I am hugging it, listening to it, wholeheartedly embracing it. By doing this, instead of wondering "Why me?" I am learning what these decades of succumbing to this illness have taught me. I am learning that it is indeed a gift. It is a teacher and I am always the ever-curious student.

I've learned that my body could be pushed to limits never imaginable and still bounce back. Even though I never thought I would return to my "typical" self, I did. I learned that with every bout of depression, I become stronger mentally and eventually physically as I push myself to beat this illness. I have learned that there will always be sad days even if I am in recovery and that I need to listen and be aware of my body's alarm system. I have learned to appreciate the simpler things in life… Something I needed to do considering the intrusive thoughts I have had. I have learned to love those around me who support me no matter what, and this circle of people has only grown over time.

I have learned that by suffering from depression a multitude of times, it has given me a few great gifts…

The gift of inspiring others… to seek out help whether from myself or their support systems and to come forward. I shed tears of happiness when I am told, "You inspired me to tell my story," or "I wanted to thank you for being such a positive role model." In my darkest days, the word "inspiration" being associated with myself would have never happened.

The gift of writing… I can't express how many words flow out of my head when I discuss my depression, anxiety, articles concerning mental illness, and images I see with inspirational messages. It has brought back the writing talent I had as a child.

The gift of explanation… to my daughter. To be able to explain mental illness to a child and have her understand is amazing. To have her still love me after explaining thoughts and feelings while ill makes me happy.

The gift of slowing down… A hard one for this alpha. I always must be doing something. It is very hard to relax for me. I have since learned to turn down added stresses in my life. I already have a full-time job, am the mother to a young girl and am PTO Treasurer for her school. I do not need any more on my plate. I have also started to meditate. It may only be four minutes a day right now, but for those four minutes I am focusing on nothing but my breaths and it feels great.

Now, instead of always thinking "Why me?" which I still do every now and then, I have turned my negativity into positivity… Now, I have begun to ask myself, "What can I do with my gift of depression? How can I help others? What has it made me realize about myself?"

Just amazing!

What I Hope to Pass on to My Daughter
August 4, 2015

WHEN I WAS PREGNANT, I had all these visions in my head of what my future child would look like. I wondered if my baby would be a boy or a girl. I wondered if he or she would have dark hair like my husband and me, blue eyes or brown, my crooked nose or his…

I also dreamt of what my baby would be like in the personality department. Shy and intelligent like my husband, outgoing and creative like myself? I never thought about whether I would pass on my history of depression to my child… not until after she was born. When postpartum depression hit, I never imagined I would survive. I didn't think my marriage would survive. Apathetic, alone, desperate and helpless, I yearned for the day that I would feel somewhat normal again, and honestly never thought I would see it. I cried. I cried oceans of tears. One day as I was sitting, sulking about how pathetic I was, the thought came to my mind… what if I passed this on to my daughter?! I didn't want to live anymore. You only want the best for your child(ren) and what happens if you passed on to them your worst!

At first, it was the postpartum depression I was worried about passing on to her. Images flashed in my mind of her huddled in a corner with tears pouring down her face repeating, "I can't! I just want to die!" with my grandchild wailing in the background. Where was I? Right next to her on the floor crying. Crying out of guilt and blame. Crying out of another bout of depression I surely would fall into. I spoke about this with my therapist and his question to me was, "What can you do if this happens?" Instead of worrying so much about a future that may or may not come true, what could I do now?

I applied this logic. I got over the fear of passing on my postpartum depression to my daughter. I was happy in thoughts with her until the next depression episode hit in 2008. It brought all those ugly thoughts and images back into my head... and new ones. Now I worried incessantly about passing on depression and anxiety in general to her. She would be screwed. Seems like with each generation, the number of times one suffered from depression increased. I now pictured her as a teenager with a knife to her wrist going back and forth in her head of whether to slice her flesh and end the pain and confusion. So much guilt built up inside of me. Years of therapy to come to terms that it may happen, but I shouldn't dwell on these thoughts.

Fast forward to this past winter, my latest and one of my most severe bouts of major depressive disorder. Once again, images flashed in my mind about passing on this horrid illness especially as my daughter is now almost nine... only five years younger than I was when first diagnosed. At this time, she has already been given an anxiety diagnosis, so my worry has already begun. Therapy for her has been a little bit helpful, but like her mother, she is stubborn and doesn't want to do the work she needs to do to develop her coping skills. Yet another thing I passed to her that I wish I didn't. Pictures in my head flash from her teenaged self, holding a knife to her wrist, to pacing her college dorm room with fingers tightly wound in her hair, to her huddled on the floor with a screaming baby and a pillow over her head trying to block out the screams. All of it seems like it will be a reality for her. I know that these images may never actually occur, but I see so much of myself in my daughter.

I gave her so many of my personality flaws... she's stubborn, strong-willed, emotional, impatient, anxious, a worrier... all these traits that have hindered and hurt me, have caused mass confusion in my brain... fireworks of thoughts, explosions, and eventually emptiness and exhaustion. Over and over and over again. Taking a positive approach to this, she has also inherited my good qualities of being caring, loving, creative, sweet, compassionate, empathetic, and silly.

If I apply the logic my therapist has told me repeatedly, "What can I do about it now?" I realize dwelling on what may be will just cause me to miss out on her life and my own. So, for now, I watch her. I watch her grow taller, smarter, more amazing. I watch that her anxiety stays under control. I research and watch for depression traits in children. I teach her about my illness and how it makes me think and act. I ask her principal at school to place her with a teacher who could handle her anxiety diagnosis. She knows she has an open-door policy with the school psychologist. She is more learned in depression and anxiety then I ever was at her age. There is more hope with her. More hope that she will recognize her triggers long before her mother ever could. Hope that she will go get help quicker because she has seen what can happen first hand.

I guess, ultimately, I hope I passed on the quality of hope to my daughter... to always feel hopeful and never to experience her mother's helplessness. My hope has conquered and won over my helplessness... a helplessness that has kicked down my door six times. My hope is my warrior. I hope I passed my warrior on to my daughter!

Calming Down
August 19, 2015

I FEEL THE ANXIETY RISING. My shoulders are stuck in an upward position. My lower back is aching. My mind has constant thoughts ping-ponging from side-to-side. My breathing becomes rapid with me needing to take several deep breaths to get enough air. I become confused, puzzled, agitated. What to do? I always have my Ativan with me. I could swallow that tiny round white pill even without water. I would relax within the next 15 minutes. Simple solution, right? I'm an alpha and my medication dependency annoys the crap out of me (but will take it if needed). Alternative solutions?

Meditation... according to the dictionary, meditation is "the act or practice of meditating" or "to think deeply or carefully about something." I've joined several Facebook Meditation groups, reading article after article on how to properly practice the art of meditation. I signed up for a free 30-day meditation program in which we were sent several four or more minute meditation verbiages. I laid down, relaxed and focused on these meditations. Some of them were wonderful, others I couldn't focus on. What I ultimately realized is that I am not a meditator.

What next...

Mandala Coloring Sheets... I had a gift card to Barnes and Noble and thought this time I should spend the money on myself instead of indulging

Sophia with another *Dork Diaries* or *My Little Pony* comic book. There, on the clearance shelves were several Mandala coloring books. I bought one for $6.98 even though I had several free printouts. There is always something about holding a real book that I enjoy. I colored and found myself entranced by the designs and the choices of colored pencils I have. Only problem… I hate to leave a picture unfinished. It took me over an hour to finish the first page.

Am I ever going to find something that will take 15 minutes or less to calm me down that isn't small, round and white?!

Rewind back to my childhood. I don't remember at what age I began, but when I would find a word, circle it, and then cross it off, I had such a sense of achievement and happiness. I would go through book after book of word searches. Could this apply to me as an adult?!

When I was in the hospital this past winter getting help for my latest, and most likely, my worst bout of depression, my father brought me a huge Penny Press book of word searches. I am a picky word search person… I will only do Penny Press books that have specialty puzzles in them. I would sit constantly with it when it was not the time for therapy and circle word after word. I blocked out all surrounding noises. I was in my own little bubble. Was this bubble linked to the word search book or the amount of medication I was receiving?

As I left the hospital and my dosages were lowered, I again found myself sitting with this book of word searches. Instantly, the bubble would engulf me. Inside this bubble, I was calm, focused. Focused on one thing, simply finding these words. It provided my brain a way to tell every other thought in my mind to "Shut the fuck up!" My brain was too busy looking for words to care about anything else. This was it, this was my way of meditating. This was my way of calming down without the need of medication in 15 minutes or less. I finally found a solution that worked for me!

I posed this question to several of my friends as everyone is different. I got a few answers:

"I will listen to calming music, read a good book, or watch silly comedies or *Tom and Jerry*. And I ask for hugs."

"I meditate and write in a journal."

"Exercise – when the body is tired, the brain can shut up and watch TV."

All great answers! There is no one answer on how to calm down. Everyone is different. I love to exercise, but I am not a runner, I hike. I do Zumba fitness classes. I mean, I HATE to run. I tried meditating and while it works for my friend, it doesn't work for me. I am just not a Zen person, as much as I would like to be. You need to pay attention to your mind. Just like medication, it is trial and error when it comes to calming down.

Now, what word was I looking for - ah yes... ACTIVITY! Shh, my bubble is forming!

Suicide
September 10, 2015

I CONTEMPLATED committing suicide when I was 18; a lot was going through my mind.

After one of many arguments concerning my birthday party, the stress of work at school, stress of the play at school (I was Stage Manager), the stress of work itself, and the large feeling of neglect, I sat in my bedroom one morning holding a case cutter (from work) in my right hand on top of the skin of my left wrist. So much was going through my mind.

Would anyone miss me?

Would anyone notice if I were gone?

Would anyone care if I were gone?

Would anyone cry at my funeral?

Was this the ideal answer to my issues?

Would anyone try to save me?

I sat there, for a good 15 minutes, repeating these questions over and over in my head. Honestly, I also thought about the huge mess it would leave on the floor. That led to the feeling that my parents would be angry with me for leaving that huge mess. Odd what you think of when you contemplate suicide.

Once I realized killing myself was not the answer, I just sat there on the floor of my room still holding the case cutter to my wrist and started to cry. It was a huge cry-fest. There was so much emotion I never knew I had in me and it was all coming out. The crying got so loud that my mother actually screamed up at me, "Steph, what's wrong?! Are you okay? You need to leave for school…" I knew I had to tell her and at this point, I was exploding in tears and words. I walked down the stairs still holding the case cutter, but now not directly over my wrist. My mom put two and two together and just started crying.

Some Dreams Just Don't Come True
September 23, 2015

WE LEARN AT A young age to follow our dreams, that all our dreams will come true... our parents encourage us, our teachers encourage us, our friends encourage us. There are so many inspiring quotes out there about it "never being too late for your dreams to come true." I've tried to listen. I've tried to believe this. But...

... some dreams just don't come true.

Growing up, I always wanted to be a mother. I saw myself having three or four children. I had names picked out for them that changed through my childhood years. I was anxious to have kids, to see if they would look at all like me, act like me.

I met my husband in my teenage prime at our first jobs. A quiet, shy boy at the time. My father wondered aloud, "You should date that studious-looking boy." Honestly, he wasn't my type. I was interested in another boy, but being that that relationship wasn't going further than friendship, I went on a date with my husband. This was back in 1996. I found him mysterious and intelligent and grew more and more to love him. We talked long before our wedding in 2004 about kids. He is an only child and enjoyed it. My mother was an only child and hated it.

I never wanted an only child. Ever. Only one child was not in my dreams. I always dreamt of more.

We talked and talked, and he eventually

convinced me that two or three was the way to go.

Our beautiful daughter, Sophia, was born in 2006. One month later, I was in short-term psych with postpartum depression and anxiety.

My husband then decided one child was enough as he became a single parent of a newborn for 12 days while working full-time over an hour away. He would not budge from this decision for a few years. As the recession hit, I agreed for the time being. We couldn't afford another child.

But dreams sit in your brain…

As we recovered from the recession and as I saw friends having babies, I wanted a second child. My husband was against me getting pregnant for fear of suffering from postpartum depression once again. We had discussed adoption before, since we both had close relatives who were adopted. He agreed, and we went to an open house at DCF on my birthday that year. After a few weeks of classes, a few months of waiting, we received our license. All we did was wait for our child.

Only about two months later we were matched. I was finally going to have my second child. The family I had always dreamed of. And he was perfect to me. A toddler full of energy (and responsibilities), curious, wanting to be loved. My love for him was instant from the first day I met him. I called him my son from that moment on.

… then the anxiety came… then the depression came… then my son was removed.

… some dreams just don't come true.

Almost a year later and I'm still blaming myself, blaming my illness. It's all my fault. I am still grieving losing him to my mental illnesses. I am still grieving losing myself to my mental illnesses. I am still grieving about losing my dream to my mental illnesses. My dream… the children I won't have. The many hugs and kisses and laughs… envisioning three rambunctious kids jumping on me. Watching them all play together and fight together. My dream, stolen from me by myself, by my depression and anxiety, my mental illnesses. A dream I have had for decades, since childhood.

Now, I am the mother of an only child, something I never wanted in my wildest dreams, and I love her deeply to infinity and beyond. She is my rock, my reason for pushing through every depressive episode. She is my funny, loving, sympathetic girl. But…

… some dreams just don't come true.

The Parent
September 30, 2015

LAST SATURDAY, my husband, my daughter and I went to BJs for our monthly shopping of meat (mainly). When we first walked into the store, my daughter, Sophia, recognized right away the song that was playing. Knowing that this song, Ed Sheeran's 'Photograph,' triggers me into thinking about T. and last winter with my anxiety and depression, she took her index fingers and stuck them in my ears. She kept them there until the song was over. This action of protection is something a parent would do.

I realized after this event occurred that in a way, I was no longer the parent. Sure, I yelled at her at times, checked her homework, made her bathe… but when it came to protection, she had the control. Reliving this event in my head after my shower on Sunday had me wrapped in a towel, sitting on the bath ledge, crying. I am supposed to be the protector. With tears rolling down my cheeks, I realized that this was not the first instance. She has been protecting me since I left the hospital in January. A little girl became Mommy to her mother.

I am the first to admit that what Sophia witnessed last winter most likely freaked her out, especially with her anxiety diagnosis. I was scaring my mother, so yes, my daughter must have been frightened. First, she had to witness my delusional talking when under numerous anxiety attacks. She

then fell victim to my many crying spells. She was at
the dinner table when I said I was too nauseous to eat
and she saw my fear of sleeping in my room. Then she
lost her brother when he went back into DCF custody,
as I was spiraling into a dark hole. After the
unthinkable happened, she had to live without me for
five days while I was in the hospital. Five days she
couldn't hug me, kiss me, or cuddle with me. She
couldn't even see me. Our only contact was over the
phone and there was a time limit.

I believe within those five days she came up
with the plan that to not lose Mommy, she needed to
protect me. When I arrived home after my
hospitalization, she would watch me with eagle
eyes. She would constantly want to be by my side. She
would repeatedly ask me, "Mommy, are you okay?" if
she saw tears in my eyes. When I would honestly
respond "no," I could see the worry in her face. That's
when she started to bring me things. If I were crying,
she would bring me a box of tissues, sit with me, hug
me and say, "It's all right Mommy, it will get
better." Just like a mother would say holding her sick
child.

At some point in these last few months, I
eventually asked her why she was so worried about
me. Her response:

"I don't want to lose you, too."

I've asked her if she misses her brother, as I am
the only one who sheds tears over this still (hence my
recent PTSD diagnosis). Her response:

"I don't want a brother anymore. I just want

my Mommy."

I am angry with myself over this. I will tell her time and time again that it is not her job to take care of me, that it is my job to take of myself and her. She still doesn't listen. She is my protector right now. In a way, I am grateful that she has become such a caring and loving and understanding person, but then I remember she is only going to be nine-years-old. Protection is not her job. Her job is to be the child; carefree, happy, exploring. Instead, she has already inherited the adult trait of protection. I am at a loss on how to correct this, so for now...

I tell her, "Sophia, it is not your job to take care of me. It is Mommy's job." And I hug and kiss her.

My Biggest Bully
October 4, 2015

AT SOME TIME in our lives everyone has been bullied. From the child with the lisp, to the kid wearing glasses, or in my case, because my maiden last name is an item of food. Kids always wanted to know if I was related to Burger King or if they can ketchup with a side of Stephanie Berger. Silly things. I was taught to brush it off, that these kids were jealous of something I had that they didn't.

I tell my daughter the same thing now as she is ridiculed for her height, tall and slender for her age. Bullying is worse now with the invention of social media. There is nowhere to hide. It makes my heart ache for my daughter.

I have a bully in my life still to this day, my biggest bully. This bully lies to me, beats me up emotionally and physically. It laughs at me almost daily and it has me questioning myself on certain things. I am never away from this bully as this bully lives in my head. My biggest bully: my depression.

I was first diagnosed as a teenager with depression. Through the decades, my depression has grown stronger and bigger like a tumor. That first episode of depression morphed through the years to major depression disorder.

As defined, MDD is "... a condition characterized by one or more major depressive episodes without a history of manic, mixed, or hypomanic episodes…" (mentalhealth.com).

In my case, we are up to six episodes. Each episode has increased my bully's evilness, has made me believe I was weak, undeserving, unworthy of love. Each time I am weakened by this bully before I can get better.

Depression lies to me. It tells me I don't deserve to be a mother. I don't deserve my friends and family. I don't deserve anything good in my life. It tells me that I am helpless. I am plankton. It tells me I shouldn't be loved, and that no one, in fact, loves me. And then it gets to the point where it tells me I shouldn't live anymore.

I have gotten to this last point a few times. I have tried to bargain with depression… if you let me live, I'll run away so I don't hurt the people I love anymore, I am not worthy of their love anyway. If you let me live, I will give in to you and do whatever you want me to, even if that means harming myself.

Depression beats me up. Emotionally, it has me crying over the blame I have for myself. It has me foggy and unable to concentrate. It has me hyperventilating and tense. And after all that, it wreaks havoc on my muscles, with physical aches in my head, shoulders, back and legs.

Depression laughs at me. Seeing my weak achy body, it laughs because it sees victory. It sees itself as a mastermind, a genius, a god. I hear its cackle first thing every morning and it still haunts me as I go to sleep.

And this bully doesn't battle alone. It has a gang right by its side. It uses its friends (anxiety, panic,

PTSD), anything to help it leech on to me longer.

I am very weak right now. Worn down. Tired. Exhausted. And empty.

Slowly, I am battling my bully. Slowly, I am becoming David to my Goliath. With medication, therapy, exercise. I will upstage my biggest bully, my depression, but it will take lots of time, and when that time comes, I know it will still be lurking around in the shadows of my brain as it is always with me waiting, just waiting for the next time.

It Finally Happened
October 18, 2015

IT FINALLY HAPPENED... a day I haven't seen in a while, even though I have been suffering from this sixth episode of depression for almost a year. I can't even remember the last time this day occurred, but today it did... the day I couldn't get out of bed.

I couldn't get up. I didn't want to. I just wanted to sleep and mope the day away with some tears and Netflix binge-watching. I didn't want to get out of bed and face the world, face my husband and child. Heck, I didn't want to face my cat. I just wanted to live in the warm bubble of my bedroom with the weight of my blankets caressing me, cradling me. Rolling over, I looked at my clock. The big hand was on the four, the little on the nine.

9:22 AM. I should have been sitting at the dining room table chatting with my husband while he cooked our weekend breakfast. I wasn't there, though. I was still in bed. Rolling onto my back I stared up at the ceiling. Emptiness. My only thought, "Wow, do I need to dust the fan blades." Somehow, I dozed off once again and awoke to my cow clock reading 10:22 AM. The cat has just opened my door and walked gracefully to the head of my bed. She jumped up and sniffed my face, rubbing her head against mine. I could hear my husband and child conversing in the dining room about breakfast.

I still didn't want to get up. I was not in any

mood to face Sunday. Just let me stay here in my bed. Don't make me move.

Jimmy approached my room and asked me what I wanted for breakfast, "Waffles or French Toast?"

I didn't care and relayed that. I really didn't. My eyes closed, opened, closed, opened, and closed. At 10:50 AM, I was told breakfast was ready. Ugh, I must get up?! I moved slowly, like a turtle to the kitchen, sat down and hunkered over my plate.

"Did you not sleep well?" asked Jimmy.

"I slept fine. I'm just having a very off day," I mumbled.

He knew what that meant. He knew that meant his wife was far away in a non-reality world. He knew she would be mopey, sad and distant the rest of the day. He knew because he has seen this so many times before.

At the end of breakfast, I schlepped upstairs to change. I forced myself to brush my teeth and hair. I threw on jeans and a hoodie and moped. I couldn't function today. I just wanted to sleep through the whole day.

Then the following words were uttered forth from my mouth, "I don't want to be alone. Don't leave me alone."

Scared at what I had just said, tears began to well up. I remember the last time those words exited my lips. I wound up putting myself into the hospital again for a few days. It worries me. Am I that person again?

We went out after, as a family, running simple errands. Sophia whined occasionally as she didn't want to stop at such boring places as Whole Foods or the liquor store. Jimmy slightly scolded her. And I, I just wished I was back in my bed, warm, passing the day away with *Orange is the New Black*, some wine and some word searches.

I Cried... Long, Hard, Delusional, Anxiety, Depression Cried

October 19, 2015
(On Stigma Fighters)

I SHOULD BE writing my book. I had absolutely nothing planned for this weekend except for book writing. It's just awful that my brain had other plans...

My brain is acting out the Civil War in my head with the South being my depression and anxiety and the North being my old self. The South won a battle last night.

A few days ago, I wrote a poem entitled "Cough, Cough, Cough..." While some might have blown off reading this poem assuming it is about having a cold, it really is about way more than that. It's about being triggered, turning into the nightmares of my recent past.

My daughter has had a cough for over a week. I knew it was taunting me, slowly pulling me back down to the emotional pit I was in. I had started to become irritated whenever I heard her cough which was plentiful at night as she would fall into slumber. By the time I went to bed, the house was silent, and all was well; until last night. I could hear her coughing. A dry hacking cough, no other symptoms. I climbed the stairs, tripping on the last two, skinning my left shin. I opened her door, and all was silent. My angelic child was sleeping. Creeping silently, I kissed her forehead and returned downstairs. I just wanted to make sure she was okay.

Through all this, I worked myself up. Was the coughing ever going to stop? Would it continue? If it did, would I get worse? Would I wind up deep in the dungeon of another depression episode when I haven't even gotten through this last one? Would the anxiety cause me to become anorexic like it did in January?

Catastrophic thoughts racing in my mind for something as simple as my daughter coughing. That is my anxiety talking. What ifs… my anxiety loves to feed off them.

Coughing… why a trigger? As I heard my daughter hacking last night, as the anxiety rose once again this week, it brought images in my brain from last December, the holidays, the hatred of weekends, of how I was, and of T. Once the last two images started playing like a DVD in my head, there was no going back. I would have to relive them and wait until the end to calm down.

I saw myself emaciated, pale, nauseous, dizzy, crying, hyperventilating, pacing, dry heaving, panicky…

I saw T., my former foster son, clueless, happy… and coughing.

He had quickly gotten a cough like any toddler who has been quarantined in a house since birth. This cough kept me awake so many nights. This cough lasted until he was removed from our house and probably hung out a bit longer. This cough was my enemy. This cough enhanced the film playing in my head.

As the scenes of the month of December and then ultimately January played out through my brain, I cried. I cried... long, hard, delusional, anxiety, depression cried. These memories stirred up bitter emotions I had quelled, or at least I thought I had. I replayed the last day I saw T., what his cheeks felt like when I held his face in my hands, his blank stare as he attempted to understand what was happening, the softness of his skin as my lips kissed his forehead. I remembered his dark hair being ruffled and exactly where we were in the house... T. standing, his back toward the dining room and me kneeling facing him. I remember what I said to him, almost a whisper as I choked down tears, "Mommy's sorry. So sorry. I love you. I will always love you." I hugged him and walked out the door.

After that, the picture changed. I was crying in my psychiatrist's office, "I don't know what else to do. I don't know what will happen if I am alone. I'm afraid to be alone." The hospital came into view, the wood doors entering me into the Behavioral Crisis Center... the screw on the lunch tray table I was planning on pushing deep into my head just to end the pain...

Twenty minutes had past. My husband was standing watching me, asking me what he could do. Myself, sitting on the sofa, crying, wiping tears from my eyes and mucous from my nose. The delusional thoughts returning... Would her coughing stop? What happens if I hear her coughing the next night? What happens if I don't sleep and my anxiety attacks worsen? What if I stop eating because I just can't fathom putting anything in my mouth? What if I need to be hospitalized again? What if I don't survive this time?

My breathing had started to get shallow. My heart began to beat slower. My tears became less. I spoke to my husband through what tears were left:

"I'm sorry. I'm so sorry. I miss him. He should be here, he should be mine. I don't think I will survive another battle with depression. I think the next time will kill me."

I was empty, empty of all emotion. Drained. In mental anguish. Still feel that way now, just empty.

Anxiety has won this battle. It is waving its confederate flag proudly. It is laughing at me, laughing loud. I am wounded, the scars internal, healing once again. I know there will be another battle to be fought, and next time I want to be on the winning end.

I Abandoned My Children: The Start of EMDR Therapy

October 23, 2015

AT THE REQUEST of my psychiatrist, I have started an alternative form of therapy called EMDR therapy. EMDR stands for eye movement desensitization and reprocessing. In basic terms, you learn to reprocess painful memories. For now, the therapist and I have only completed my intake and documented that my eyes can indeed follow his fingers (this latter function is a major step for EMDR). The first week was mainly an introduction; after all, we have never met before. It took me weeks to find an EMDR therapist in my area who had an opening and took my insurance. He made me feel comfortable and hopeful in this new form of therapy, so I decided I would stick with him. Where that leaves me with my CBT (Cogitative Behavioral Therapy) therapist is a question that will remain without an answer for a while.

Week two, this past Monday, I arrived right after seeing my psychiatrist. It was a "Stephanie really needs her head examined" type of day. Going to my psychiatrist already works me up as I pass so many triggering landmarks to her office from work... DCF, the way I would take to T.'s daycare, the hospital, the ER entrance to the hospital...

So, I arrive already full of emotion.

"Today," he states, "We're going to target certain memories that are the most powerful and that yield the most feeling for you. These will be used when we start the actual EMDR step."

Okay, no problem, I got this. I start explaining the last day with T. for me. Tears were forming in my eyes. I was getting choked up. I began to stare off at his orchids. Glancing back at my therapist, I could see he noticed how triggering this was.

His response, "Perfect. This is definitely one memory we will use. Can you think of any others that you think are intertwined with this one? Maybe you might not realize it yet. Try to think of one."

My whole memory of my last day with T.... myself in constant tears, shaking, tensing muscles in my hands, rocking back and forth, in a delusion talking to myself... seeing me at my worst or what I thought was my worst... then admitting defeat, that the only way for me to live would be for me to remove myself from the house, led to a whole other set of emotions for leaving my children. Leaving my daughter and my foster-to-adopt son who wasn't even three and utterly clueless as to why his new Mommy was leaving him. This ultimately led to me admitting a feeling, the worst feeling a mother could have for her children... Abandonment. I abandoned him that night. Yes, it was ultimately the best decision for everyone, but for me as a mother, I felt that I abandoned him. In my mind, I feel as though I didn't try hard enough to keep him with us. Even though I was on the verge of losing myself completely, abandoning him led to the deepest depression I have ever been through. A depression that like Hurricane Ivan in 2004, re-spawned itself recently.

A mother never abandons her child!

And then I did it again. I abandoned Sophia when I put myself in the hospital a couple of weeks later. I left her without even saying goodbye. Upon realizing I could not see her while staying at the hospital, the abandonment feelings came full force and my tears could not stop. I was crazy hysterical. Those were the longest days I've had in my adult life. My daughter is one of my biggest sources of strength and I was without her physically for days. I abandoned her... AGAIN!

Bingo! Apparently, my demons from my bad mental health days were not all buried or squashed. I spoke to the therapist, "I abandoned my daughter. I abandoned her when I experienced postpartum depression exactly one month after she was born. I was hospitalized for it and was there for almost two weeks. Even though I could see her, I still abandoned her."

I spoke up again, "I missed so many days of her life at that moment. She was only four weeks when I admitted myself and I was there for 12 days!"

It doesn't matter, in my head, knowing this is what I had to do. I had to "abandon" both her and T. to get better. Instead, my brain continues the flow of abandonment with what if Sophia was a foster child, would I have given her back too?! Would I have abandoned her permanently?! Even worse, I did, in fact, have a plan to leave. If I'd had a place to run to, I would have been gone. I would have abandoned her and my husband.

The therapist spoke, "These two situations are definitely linked. You have some powerful emotions linked to both that are the same. Can you dig further into your past and come up with something from your childhood that you think could be a possible trigger for both?"

That is where the story ends. I thought for a while, but I had a relatively happy childhood. I never felt abandoned as a young child. I replied to him by shrugging and saying, "No, there is nothing else."

He explained that this was okay. If there are old hidden memories, they may come up during the actual EMDR therapy. I often wonder if there is anything else there that I've made myself forget.

I left his office completely emotionally drained. I had not been home in roughly 12 hours. I walked through my front door looking straight at my husband and my beautiful daughter, and yet I still had strong emotions that I did abandon her, questioning if I will ever forgive myself.

Tick, Tick, Tick

November 3, 2015

I AM SITTING HERE, antsy, ants in my pants, internally shaking. I know it is coming, but I don't know when. The ticking time bomb inside of me. When will this geyser blow? When will I have a complete mental breakdown? I can feel it, feel the bubbling within. I'm writhing in my chair. I can't focus. My breathing is quick and shallow. An anxiety attack that will most likely continue, on and off for the rest of the day, for many days.

I woke up this morning with a heavy heart after therapy last night. Hearing Jimmy and Sophia talk about our time with T. in the house… hearing them say they missed him. It was helpful after they have cautiously tip-toed around me trying to avoid those stubborn painful Lego pieces of my brain. I needed to hear it. I needed to know I was human with all my emotions. My husband was hopeful, saying he could see the person T. was turning into. He could see our family of four. He wanted to try to make it work. My anxiety and panic ruined that. Hearing him say he could not handle the two kids, his full-time job, and me. It was an emotional blade that kept stabbing me with guilt and anger toward myself. Hearing him say he was frustrated because he didn't know what to say to me, trying to avoid triggering me, knowing logic wouldn't work.

All this I appreciated and only made me love

him more but, on the flipside, made me self-loathe more. Hearing him say that right after T. left the house when he was hoarding all the toys and items into T.'s old bedroom was painfully hard, sent more heartache. But I wanted to know. I needed to know. I wanted to know he felt something. I wanted to know that they both felt something.

It isn't just the heavy heart. I can't stop moving. My fingers keep wiggling, fists clenching. I keep slithering around. My heart is rapidly beating. I know it is coming. Something I desperately fear, the mental breakdown. Unsure of what it will bring as I already spend most days with anxiety attacks and tears.

I need to subside my fears, to disconnect the ticking clock, but my incredible amount of guilt lies in the way. I know what I need to do. I need to call in sick, for a mental health day. I need a moment to break this Deja-Vu routine. A day where I put myself first. But, my guilt is strong. Guilt... Stigma... I'd feel guilty because I am not physically ill. No fever, no headache, no vomiting. What some would view as a day of freedom, even call me a liar, although that day would most likely consist of me in bed, maybe taking a hike. What am I so afraid of? Work knows my history. My brain is ill and at times it needs to rest, yet I don't allow it to. As if a different outcome would arise this time, as if it could all just vanish; I am foolish to think that. My illnesses have only gotten worse with age. Come on, Stephanie, why would you think this time would be different?!

Tick, tick, tick... still can't focus, still shaky...

tick, tick, tick... Go home Stephanie, you need the break... tick, tick, tick...

I'm Trapped
November 10, 2015

FIVE DAYS A WEEK, I am good. Some of those days are better than others, some worse. All of them end poorly; they end at my house. My house, a place that use to provide safety and comfort, is now a place I hate being in. It has become my anxiety's favorite clubhouse, a place where it decides to throw dance parties. And the last two days of the week, Saturday and Sunday, I attempt to leave, but have nowhere to go. Errands do not need to be run. The rain prevents any outdoor activity. I'm trapped. No hopes of escaping for another year and a half when we move to get Sophia into a better school system for Middle School.

I despise going home. I feared it to an extreme a year ago. I would cry, in silence, when it was time to leave work. The darkness outside only mirrored the fear that grew within me. At home was where all the tension was. It was where all the noises were. It was where my children, my newly born annoyances, were. I can't allow my mind to go there. At bedtime, my anxiety became Goliath. What noises would I hear tonight that would keep me awake? Would I hear coughing? Would T. wake me? Would Sophia wake me? Ugh, the heat just turned on... I just want to sleep. I NEED to sleep. All would be better if I slept.

Sleep didn't come for a long while. I thought once T. was removed I would return to my normal sleeping habits. Problem was, although T. left, my anxiety took residence. It remained as strong as before. I was only growing weaker, submissive. Every morning, I woke up gagging when I opened my eyes. Every night, I shook out of fear of this house. This house that my husband and I bought so our family could grow, so Sophia would have a yard to play in. This house I used to love so much.

I still hate it. It still hasn't kicked out the one resident that was never invited to stay. That relative you so desire to leave but doesn't. I force myself to go home. A bit easier now than a year ago, but I still need to force myself there. The nights are still full of anxiety. I still take medication to subside it, but it is still there. There are no sounds from that bedroom right across the hall, only the residual ones that play in my head. The heat still turns on. The neighbors still come home late and slam doors. The dogs outside still bark to each other, carrying on a conversation. And I still fear it all. I still sit wanting to plug up my ears. If only I didn't hear all this.

I sleep with earplugs. I have for years. They go into my ears when I decide to roll over and sleep. Before that time, my ears would hear the world while reading and watching shows on the Kindle. In addition, they hear the overwhelming voice of my anxiety, that gripping annoying tone that forces you to listen. That is something the earplugs will never cover up. I just want to yell at it, to just shut up for once, to leave me alone. I want it to take a vacation, travel the world, but it doesn't.

I turned everything off, put my earplugs in my ears and went to sleep. Tossing and turning, brain overloading with racing thoughts. Geez, just shut up already! I turn toward my clock, close to an hour has passed. Ugh! Not again. Knowing I shouldn't stay in bed, at least all those doctors say not to, I rise and go down to the basement. Laying down on the loveseat, with the cat curled into me, a throw on my legs, I watch a show from DVR. One more hour I'll lose of sleep. So many hours wasted.

I've let my anxiety in. I've embraced that it doesn't want to leave. I'm so drained of fighting it. I give up. You can stay. You can keep me awake. You can do what you want to me. Just take away the fear of my home. Let me enjoy my evenings and weekends. Let me enjoy the occasional day or two with my family. Let me live again already. You've trapped me, and I want my freedom. I want to have control again.

Grateful
November 27, 2015

AS THANKSGIVING PASSES and we all take time to think about what we are grateful for, who we are grateful for, I am reminded that being grateful has a whole other meaning when talking with anyone who has a mental illness.

Sure, I am extremely grateful for my beautiful, caring, intelligent daughter. I am grateful for my husband who took his wedding vows seriously and has stood by me through hell several times in the last 19 years. I am grateful for my parents who helped me and advocated for me instead of abandoning me. But, what am I most grateful for?

I am most grateful to be alive. I am grateful I didn't slash my wrists 17 years ago. If I had done that, my daughter would not exist today. There would not be the light in many people's lives that is Sophia Faye. There would be no blue-eyed, dirty-blonde-Hermoine hair. There would be no sweet smiles and daily kisses. She would not be here because I would not be here. If I slashed my wrist then, I not only would have killed myself, I would have killed her.

I am grateful I did not run away nine years ago. I am grateful I could not think of where to run away to because that kept me home. It kept my husband and me together. It kept me with my daughter. It kept me from missing so many firsts in her life including her first word, "Mama," at 10 months old. If I had run away, I would have missed her first step, her first real hug, her first day of school and eventually her high school graduation, marriage and any future grandchildren.

I am grateful I did not gain access to that screw on the lunch tray table in the Behavioral Crisis Center last January. If I did, it would have pierced my skin and gone into my head. I could've caused myself extreme damage that would have made my daughter motherless. It would have caused her so much pain, years of psychotherapy and possibly hospitalizations. She would feel the grieving I felt then and so much more... the grieving I still feel now. I would have given my only ever supportive husband a vegetable for a wife. I would have extolled my pain, guilt and anger on the people I love the most in this world who have only ever supported me.

As we all sat just a day ago, going around the table saying what we are grateful for, these are the things I instantly thought of... not completing suicide, not running away, not giving myself a lobotomy. The real answers of someone with a mental illness. But when it was my turn I said, "I am grateful for my loving supportive family."

The Room of Requirement: EMDR Continued

December 11, 2015

I'VE RECENTLY STARTED a new form of therapy, switching from my years of CBT to EMDR therapy. This is a whole new ballgame. Where CBT would try to train me to constantly think positively about myself by saying positive things into a mirror, EMDR is tricking my brain into rethinking that way as to erase all the negative thoughts I have about myself concerning T. last year and concerning Sophia with postpartum and last year. It is not an easy feat for someone who, for almost 36 years, has always been extremely self-critical and lives with an inner bitch. This inner bitch is very cruel.

EMDR started like any other form of therapy with intake questions. Then we went over the "calm down" exercises. One of these would be performed at the end of each session to calm any anxiety brought about during the session. One such "calm down" exercise is "The Container Exercise." For this, you picture a container in which you can put the highly emotional thoughts discussed away until the following session. After describing this to me, the first thing I thought of was The Room of Requirement from *Harry Potter*. J.K. Rowling knew what she was doing with this room. The Room of Requirement is only accessible when someone has a real need for it, filled with everything the seeker is searching for.

It is pictured as a room filled with discarded items previous owners have tossed away. Not only is it full of junk, but important items have been thrown out due to being too powerful; just like my memories and emotions.

It was after my first true EMDR session using bilateral stimulation (tracking my therapist's fingers from right to left) that he chose this "calm down" exercise. Problem was, he missed a step, the step about me NOT entering the room. Here I am, eyes closed, staring in a room like the picture above with piles and bookshelves of stuff, Tchotchkes. I am poised in front of a wooden bookshelf about six feet tall. It is made of thick rough wood, chunky, but worn. There are a variety of things already on this bookshelf... a diadem, books, a golden snitch... and other various items from the Harry Potter world. From the corner of my right eye, I can see the vanishing cabinet Draco Malfoy used and in the corner of my left eye, a Gothic arched opening. I am intrigued by this opening but need to finish the task at hand.

"Place those memories in the Room of Requirement," my therapist says. I take a metallic box, like a small treasure chest and put it on the shelf directly in front of me. "Now close the door to the room."

Trouble arises. "I can't," I say, "I'm stuck!"

He seems slightly perplexed by my statement and asks me to describe further.

"My feet are fused to the floor. They can't move. It's like a magnetic force is holding me to this spot."

He thinks a moment. "Hmmm… it seems that maybe you can't leave these memories behind, that you are too attached to them for now."

What started out as a calming exercise, now became an anxiety-inducing one! We tabled this exercise for the following week.

So, this past Monday, as I am following his finger from the right to the left, I find myself back in the Room of Requirement. I am still fused to that spot with my treasure chest of emotions and memories in front of me, but my eyes are very much focusing on the sunlight coming from the gothic arched opening. I can turn my head toward it slightly seeing the royal blue skies with the cumulus clouds, rays of sunshine casting shadows over the cold stone floors.

"Do you feel safe in this room?" he starts.

"Yes, although cold in nature, I am calm."

"Do you hear anything? Can you see anything else?" my therapist asks, still moving his fingers.

"I can hear Sophia laughing outside the opening."

"What do you think that means?"

And the epiphany… "Happiness lies outside this room. My daughter, the sun, the fresh air."

"Can you move?"

As I glance back into my mind, I realize that my feet have shifted to the left toward this opening. "I haven't lifted up my feet, but I shifted toward the opening."

"That's a great start! You moved."

Of course, I didn't see this as overly wonderful, what's shifting an inch or two in one direction, but then again, I live with an inner bitch, so naturally I would not see this as amazing.

"I wonder, though, why you feel so safe in this room when you know happiness lies outside that opening?" My therapist states.

Safe… was safe the best term? Was it more that I felt comfortable? Why did I find this dark place so relaxing?

And then an answer hit me:

"I have been attached to these emotions for so long I do not think I can part from them yet, as much as I want to be happy. I know that there is so much work left to do, and I don't want my family to see this part of me, so it is better it is hidden and fused in this room."

"What part of you is this?"

"The evil Stephanie."

Letting Go
December 31, 2015

NEW YEAR'S EVE...

A time of reflection of the year that is about to end and the time to make promises or resolutions to the year about to start.

What do you see when you stand and look in the mirror? The reflection of yourself? Is it a positive or negative reflection? As I stood in the bathroom getting ready for work this morning, it was hard to see a good person staring back at me...

A year ago, to the day, was the last time I saw my little boy.

I knew this day would come, probably the most painful memory surrounding that time. I didn't realize how quick it would get here. There were months of anxiety attacks leading up to today knowing it was coming, months of therapy to help me, and months of thinking, lots of thinking.

I can see him, standing in front of me, looking at me, his "Mommy." I can't help but cry, salty tears slowly dripping from my eyes, gravity forcing them down my cheeks and eventually falling off my face. He is just staring, curious, probably repeating in his head, "What is wrong with Mommy?" I am holding his hands in my own, feeling his skin. I bring each one up to my lips and kiss them. His deep sienna eyes following my movements saying, "What is going on?" Then I place my hands on his plump cheeks and caress them, trying to brand the feeling into my brain forever. Soft, very soft. I cup his face and bring the teary mess of my own close to his. I kiss his forehead, his nose, his cheeks, his chin. Then I back away repeating, "I'm sorry, so sorry. Mommy is so sorry, T. Mommy loves you and will always love you." I turn to leave knowing my little boy is longing to know where Mommy is going.

Pain, anguish, heartbreak. They all take over my reflection in the mirror. Soon they are joined in with guilt, failure, misery. How has it been a year? Three hundred and sixty-five days have passed? Where was I?

During therapy this week, I had a realization. As a depressive, I am automatically prone to dwelling in the past, kind of like I am stuck, my feet bound in a pool of molasses. I can't move, I am etched into this memory. What has staying in the past done? I've missed so many important and great memories with my present daughter because my brain just wasn't here. It chose to be absent, it chose to be in purgatory. Of course, telling me to get my head out of the ass of my past and join the present day is so much easier said than done. Remember, I am a chronic depressive. I am used to living in the past, so used to it, I don't know what it is like to live in the present. But in therapy this week, holding the hand buzzers for my EMDR treatment, I finally realized I NEED to let go. I need to pry myself from December 31, 2014, and move on for the health of everyone, especially myself.

How do I let go? How do I let go and not forget

the terrific boy that T. was (and probably still is)? How do I let go of leaving him because I failed him? Because I failed myself? How do I let go of sliding down into the depths of hell so quickly and still ignoring it? How will I forgive myself for all of this? For everything that was never supposed to happen again?

During this therapy session, when closing my eyes for another round of EMDR, I pictured Mahatma Gandhi, or was it the Buddha? All I know is it was a bald seated figure in shrouds. My therapist thought it interesting but not strange that I pictured this. He wanted to know why. I replied, saying I felt they were the epitome of being calm and relaxed, the epitome of acceptance. He then had me close my eyes to ask this figure how I could let go. I was anxious for a response. I could see in my head standing next to them and asking them, "How can I let go but not forget? How can I live in the present?"

A minute passed. I opened my eyes and took a deep breath. My therapist asked what happened. "They didn't tell me anything. I spent the last minute asking, begging out of desperation, and nothing."

"That's okay," he said, "Realizing you need to let go is a start and we will work from there."

So, December 31st, 2015, I am letting go of your older sister. I will try my hardest to throw away the horrible emotions my depression has associated with her. I will embrace my little boy in my memories and leave the pain and guilt there. It will not be instant. This will be a process, but I have finally made a step in the correct direction.

My Husband
February 24, 2016

TWENTY YEARS AGO, two teenagers met at their
first jobs. We were young and naïve, carefree. He was
the quiet, careful boy, with a mysterious air about him.
He rarely ever spoke, but somehow worked himself
into our small little click at Bradlees. We were a group
of teenagers who thought we were too cool by hanging
out in the parking lot after the store closed. I never had
any thought of dating him, thinking he was not "my
type." At that point I was into bad boys, specifically
shoplifters in my lack of judge for character. But life
has a way of twisting things into your favor, even if
you don't realize it. I like to blame my father for this
one as he suggested I date the studious looking stock
boy, but also intertwined into this was the fact that I
was in a dating drought, and the boy I wanted to date
at the time, my best male buddy, did not reciprocate
those feelings and in addition, suggested I go out with
James.

James was more than shy. He lurked in the
shadows, my shadows, and rather thinking that was
creepy, I was more curious about him than ever. The
mystery that surrounded him made him more
appealing, more desirable to my then 16-year-old self.
After receiving an e-mail from him where he wanted
to "save himself the embarrassment of asking me
outright," he asked me out and I said yes. Our first date
we went to see *Romeo & Juliet* with Claire Danes and

Leonardo DiCaprio and then had dinner at Friendly's.

We grew close and even survived a year of a long-distance relationship when he started college and I was still in my senior year of high school. I was accepted at the University of Maryland and joined him there the following year, much to my parents' dismay. Being a parent now, I can understand their frustration. I can't fathom allowing my daughter to follow her boyfriend to college. We were engaged in the spring of 2000 after dating for almost four years. We were advised to finish college and find jobs if we wanted assistance in paying for the wedding. We wed four years later, on a stunning day in early September.

At the point of our wedding, James, who I now refer to as Jimmy, had witnessed two of my depressive episodes, being caught in the web of one of them. I was outright cruel to him. Slammed doors in his face, hit him, said horrible things, but he stayed. He stayed because he knew it wasn't the real me. He helped me escape my toxic behaviors that I learned from my mental illness. He was my greatest support, but I was only just beginning to see how wonderful he was.

In 2006, we became pregnant, something we both wanted very much. We had always discussed children before and we planned on two to three via pregnancy and/or adoption. My pregnancy was blissful. I was glowing daily. I loved being pregnant, it made me feel feminine, breaking my tomboy nature. Our daughter was born that October. We were so happy, until I wasn't a few weeks later. My health, both mental and physical, rapidly deteriorated. Then, the hospitalization happened. My husband had to take care of our daughter and continue to work full time over an hour away for 12 days by himself. He woke very early, fed Sophia, changed her, dressed for work, dropped her off at my parents and went to work. After work, he traveled an hour and a half, picked Sophia up from my parents and brought her to the hospital to visit with me. This is all after I consistently told him he could do better. I told him to leave me and take Sophia, to find someone who could be a better, stable wife and mother. I yelled at him to leave.

But he stayed.

He stayed in 2008, when I went through my next major depressive episode. And again, he stayed in 2014 even after my mental illness caused us to lose our foster son back to child services. The latter episode was the most painful I have experienced. This man cared for our daughter, our foster son, and me for over a month. I was the third child. Through everything that has happened, he has never blamed me. He blames himself for not being able to keep up with his full-time job and take care of all of us.

I've asked him, many times, why he stays, why he stays with someone who has caused so much heartache? His answer has never changed:

"Because I love you and you make things interesting!"

With this, I know I am truly blessed.

The Summer Breeze

March 2, 2016

THIS PAST WEEKEND I attended a mental health first aid course and am proud to say I am now certified. We were deeply educated in the topic of suicide and self-injury, as that was one of the most cautious illnesses to deal with. During the focus on suicide, several things started to swirl into my mind, mostly focused on when I held a case cutter to my wrist 18 years ago.

It is widely known that thoughts of suicide and attempts are experienced by teens and young adults with many ideas first sparking even in one's childhood. Teenagers, with their raging hormones are prone to depression and anxiety, the main precursor to suicidal thinking. I was 14 when I was diagnosed with my first episode of depression. Fourteen; the same age that a young teen took her life when I was a senior in high school. This was the same year I held that case cutter. I know everything that was swirling through my head at that age and I didn't cut myself, what was going through her head?

All of this got me thinking though, was this really my first experience with depression? Was 18 my first experience with suicidal thoughts?

In Junior High (also known as middle school), we had talents we were sorted into. It was a school for the "gifted and talented." You needed to submit work proving you should be at this school. I was waitlisted and then received acceptance into their creative writing program. Writing was my passion as a pre-teen. I have always found love writing stories and especially poetry. Every year, at the end of the year, our creative writing talent put out anthologies called "My Third Eye."

I still have them in my possession.

The first one I was in is dated June 1992. I was 12 and puberty hadn't graced me with its presence yet. I learned in this first aid course that a warning sign of suicide is writing about, well, suicide and death. It is listed in the handbook. This worried me as I was reading my contribution to "The Third Eye" that year:

The Summer Breeze

A summer breeze
Passes by.
A young woman cries,
She cries of death,
Death of her friend,
She roams and wades in the water,
She fills her brain of secrets,
Secrets too big to tell,
She closes her eyes,
And thinks,
Of her friend,
Who has passed away,
A tear hits the water,
And she screams,
It should have been me!

I was 12, writing about death, and this poem was modified from the original. The line "Who has passed away," read more like, "Who killed herself." No one read this as a warning sign of anything back in 1992. They read this poem and thought it was wonderfully written and chose this as my entry for the anthology. Of course, in 1992, who wanted to discuss preteen/teen depression?! Who spoke of preteen/teen suicide?! Mental illness was still very taboo and honestly, how many preteens/teens were even thinking about it?!

I tried to think what would have caused me to write this at such an early age. The only things I can remember is that I was starting a new school with new people as this was not my zoned school, and the death of my grandfather. As I re-read this poem though, now living through my mental illness history, I am skeptical to believe I wrote this because my grandfather died. Although I grieved his passing, we weren't very close in life.

Reading this again, I am looking at it with the eye of a mother of a preteen girl and I am worried. I am worried for her. Middle school is so much worse than it used to be (thank you, technology and social media). What she will have to endure makes my heart ache now. With my diagnosis, I have gained an intuition on what signs to look for with her and am grateful for that. I just don't want to be reading a poem like this penned from her 12-year-old hand. A poem like this would worry me. That last line echoes in my

mind, "It should have been me!" …
    "It should have been me!"

Hello, God, It's Me, Stephanie

March 21, 2016

I AM BY NO MEANS a religious person. I grew up in a very reformed Jewish household where we exchanged presents for Hanukkah, but aside from that, there was very little else we did. At one point, I did want to extend my Hebrew education and attended a year of Hebrew school. I did exceptionally well. The option was presented to me on having either a Bat Mitzvah or a Sweet 16. I chose the latter, not knowing that we were moving, nor that Sweet 16s were not a big deal outside of the NYC area. Once we moved out of the melting pot of Brooklyn, I didn't tell people I was Jewish. Like my mental illness, stigma and prejudice were surrounding it.

I met my husband at 16. He grew up attending Catholic churches on Christmas and Easter. His father attended Catholic School as a child and decided it wasn't for him. Jimmy and I are not religious people. There was no debate on which religion our child(ren) would follow because we both didn't follow any. Respectively, I tend to acknowledge myself as Agnostic while my husband says he's an Atheist. In fact, Sophia is more religious than we are, as she believes in God.

When 9/11 happened or 12/14 (Sandy Hook), while others found God, I digressed even further wondering how could a God kill these innocent children? I am extremely respective to all those who are devout in their religion. I find myself at times jealous of these kinds of people. I hold the First Amendment in high regards; freedom of speech, freedom of religion, and freedom of the press. Everyone should be allowed to believe what they want because honestly, if we all believed the same thing, this world would be terribly boring.

I know, I know, where am I going with this?

Last Saturday I went on a hike in my second backyard, a huge park with hiking trails literally down the street from my house. Unless I am hiking with friends or family, I usually zone out, focusing on the sights, smells and sounds of nature. On this such occasion, I was presented with something interesting. I started up the hill to walk through the hay-fields and opposing me, coming down the hill, was a college-aged female with a backpack and headphones on. I thought nothing of it. I pass so many people on the trails, especially on such a beautiful day as it was. I do tend to observe people, whether it is because they are being loud or just for the sheer fact that they are wearing flip flops on a pebble and root filled trail. The gap between the woman and I was closing. She looked at me, reached into her pocket, and pulled out a rectangular slip of paper.

As we passed, she handed me the slip of paper and said, "You look like you could use this. Hope you have a great day."

My initial inspection of the slip of paper was, "Holy cow, she handed me money!"

Of course, I didn't believe that. I mean it was a

$1,000,000 bill, how many of those are there in the world? Do they even actually exist? Do they have Ben Franklin on them? Then I looked further at the words scrawled on the paper:

"God will never leave you."

What made me stand out? Could she really read my eyes from far away? Could she see the inner turmoil I've been going through? Did God tell her? Oh my, does that mean there is a God or another higher being? For some reason, she knew something was wrong and taking a small part out of her day, she brought a smile to my face.

A stranger cared enough to make me smile.

Now I am beginning to wonder, are there spiritual signs? Signs that show us there are other people looking out for us even when we can't fathom the thought of looking after ourselves? Do these signs come from messages from a God, from deceased family and friends? Do we have guardian angels? Or is it just the sheer fact that I looked sad, this co-ed picked up on it and thought that maybe if I attended church, I would gain a great group of friends and a spirituality I certainly lacked…

Sophia Scared
March 30, 2016

AT AGE SIX, I brought my daughter in to her pediatrician for her yearly physical. This was not the first year that the doctors questioned me about her hysterics when they would get within two feet from her. I kept telling myself that is normal child behavior, most kids fear the doctor. The prior year's physical went by with them questioning me about her and noting, "White Coat Syndrome," in her file.

We thought nothing of it until the following year.

The physician's assistant who saw Sophia at six was the same one who performed her physical the year before. There were many tears, screams, and full on hysterics once Sophia and I arrived at the doctor. I was only hoping this year they put in that mini-bar I so needed. The tears started small as we sat in the waiting room. Once we were brought back into the examination room, Sophia's fears were escalated, and she was shaking, screaming, crying, saying, "No, no doctor, no," repeatedly. I feared the other children in the waiting area were hearing this and their poor parents would be blaming me for a newly instilled fear in their children.

I sat and watched my child. What was making her like this? Did she remember the shots she received last year because she was going to start school? I tried calming her, rocking her shaking little torso in my own telling her that there would only be the flu shot. This didn't quell her fears. Her crying was to the point where she was about to vomit. When the PA came in, she remembered Sophia right off the bat without even looking at her file first. She tried to comfort her in a voice that only pediatricians, daycare and young school age teachers have. That sweet tenderness, comforting.

Through the screams, because Sophia was doing anything but calming down, the PA asked me several questions about her behavior. Did she do this often or only with doctors? Did she fear other things to this extreme? Did she complain of being sick? My child was the queen of stomach aches. Every day she told me she had a stomach ache. I just brushed it aside. Then she asked, "Is there a history of childhood anxiety in the family?"

"Not childhood, but both my husband and I have a history of anxiety."

And so, the PA tentatively gave Sophia the diagnosis of generalized anxiety disorder and suggested therapy.

As it turned out, unbeknownst to me, both my mother and my husband were anxious children.

What kind of therapy do young children have? Luckily this occurred around parent/teacher conferences and within one week, Sophia's first grade teacher had recommended her for the 'Special Friends' program. This program was heaven-sent. Once a week, Sophia was taken to a room with her 'Special Friend' (an adult aide) to color, play games and talk. That one time a week was exactly what she needed.

And then she aged out. Third grade hit and with that, her anxiety grew. She now had intense fears of becoming sick. The first instance was told to me by the school nurse. Sophia came to her after hearing a new kid with a lisp. She was hysterical and thought that she would get one too, that she would develop one instantaneously. The next day, her afternoon care person called my husband to pick her up because she couldn't stop crying. A boy fell on the playground and had a bloody nose. Like a switch, the hysterics started, and she had to be picked up because she was scaring the other kids thinking she would 'catch' the bloody nose.

We found a therapist that specialized with childhood anxiety and brought her. Sophia took weeks to talk about things, and until she did, everything got worse. It could be any moment, something so minuscule to the rest of us was a giant shit storm to her and you had mere seconds to calm her before the storm hit. She became Sophia Scared.

When Ebola was in the news, of course Sophia was old enough to read and comprehend what was being said on the radio, she was eight, she was so worried about catching it. I had planned to take her into NYC for a day during Spring Break to go to the American Girl Doll store. She wouldn't go. Once she heard a doctor in NYC had Ebola, she would not budge from this decision and cried incessantly about it. Even after I showed her articles that the doctor was okay, it took a couple weeks of therapy before she started to change her mind. We did go to NYC, but I swear she kept looking over her shoulder often.

Her latest major episode occurred last August. We were on vacation on a campground and several dogs were roaming the land. One had a collar and tags and the other didn't. We had to lasso these dogs while the campground owner called the dogs' owner. Seems this happened quite often. Sophia let the dogs lick her and then someone had to bring up rabies. Sophia flipped out, shaking, crying, talking silly, as I tried to calm her.

"Sophia, the dogs don't have rabies. Their owners live next to the campground. They are coming to get them."

Through sobs, "But I let them lick me! I have rabies, I know it!"

My final attempt, "Sophia, did the dog bite you? Are you bleeding? No, then you don't have rabies."

And we spent the next 20 minutes waiting for her episode to pass.

That was the thing with Sophia Scared, we never knew how long the episodes would last. It could be five minutes or it could be over an hour (we had a couple that were over an hour). I admit, my initial responses were not the best solutions. I screamed at her pretty loudly, so she could hear me over her screams. I ignored her. I tried to reason with her. I became frustrated with her and myself because nothing I did helped. Ultimately, the best we could do was weekly therapy and waiting for her bout to pass before calmly speaking with her.

Over the last few months, Sophia Scared has been put on the back burner. She hasn't had therapy in about a year and is doing well. She is now Sophia Survived.

Not One Smile
April 4, 2016

FOR THE LAST MONTH or two during EMDR therapy, my therapist has tried very hard to penetrate the rock-solid protection I keep around my postpartum memories. These memories were so deeply buried that the strongest jackhammer wasn't getting to them. We had made brief success by making me realize I need to have compassion for my Postpartum self and I am beginning to, but the more hurting, the rawer, the more emotional memories, were still very much deeply buried.

It was in one such session, I did slip out that I had never grieved over that period. I never grieved for myself or for Sophia. I never let myself unravel for never getting a typical postpartum period. I never lamented the lack of love I had for my baby. Ultimately, my deeply buried memories were rising to the surface themselves; my therapist was the grave digger exhuming them. When discovering this, he told me to take some time at home alone with pictures during that first year and let the mourning begin. Because I have been so busy, this did not occur until yesterday.

I arose yesterday already feeling different. A few days of happiness, or I should say contentment, are usually followed by a few anxiety-filled days or, in this case, depression-filled days. I was off. Irritability crept in early followed by sadness, anger, hypervigilance and the worst, emptiness. I faked any idea of normality yesterday. Since I had some spare time, I figured I would create a graphic to use for the upcoming Postpartum Support Walk to try to ignite donations, using myself as the victim. I sat at my laptop and opened the file under Pictures labeled "Sophia Faye." I then proceeded to open the folders labeled "2006" and "2007." With each picture I glanced at, my eyes welled up with tears until finally they exploded.

For the first year of Sophia's life, there is not one picture of me with her where I am smiling. Not one smile…

The pictures start two months after her birth. I have no pictures of her and I those first two months except for the day she was born. Because my mental illness was rapidly increasing in those first two months, pictures were the farthest thing from my mind. But because of this, I have no way of remembering her first Halloween, nor her first Thanksgiving. All I remember during those two months is how many times I had to visit my therapist and psychiatrist and ultimately, how I ended up in the short-term psychiatric ward at the hospital. I wish I could remember her coos, her smiles caused by gas, just her.

After these first two months, there are sporadic photos of me holding Sophia. As I held her, looking into my eyes, you can see how drugged up I was, how emotionless I was. My fake smile was more like a smirk. I was acting the part of mother and I was doing horribly bad at it. Over the next few months, the strung-out face starts to fade, and the smirk becomes slightly fuller... trying hard to be a smile, but it isn't. My eyes, instead of looking like an addict, look blank and empty. I am tempting the photographer to see the real me while attempting to cover it up.

Months and months, still not one smile, one REAL smile.

It wasn't until I came across a photo from September 2007, 11 months after Sophia was born, where my eyes were happy. They sparkled, twinkled, danced, while I held my daughter. Eleven months I spent tragically suffering from no emotion, from a type of death, from crippling postpartum illnesses. I stared at this photo in more detail. Still mostly a smirk on my face, but it slightly resembled a smile. There was some emotion behind it. I was not a zombie anymore. I was not a robot anymore. I was human again.

Eleven months I spent living a hell where my brain was playing the devil. Eleven months I spent acting out motherly duties to take care of my daughter, but not remembering or even caring about any of it. Eleven months I spent looking at my daughter wondering why I was her mother instead of someone "normal," she deserved so much more.

These pictures, these memories, were buried for many reasons deep within me. They are hard to process. Not loving your child and being able to see it on your own face is something I wish no mother must ever go through. I lost that time when Sophia was just beginning to discover the world around her. I can't get it back and I will never have that opportunity again. For this, I mourn, I grieve, I ache.

Eleven months, and not one smile.

EMDR, PPD, & Self-Compassion
April 9, 2016
(On Stigma Fighters)

EVERY MONDAY I have my therapy appointment. This is for my new therapy that I started a few months ago, EMDR. If I tried to explain the exact technique, I think I would confuse you further. What I can say, is that it is hard. It was extremely hard in the beginning recounting memories that often brought me to tears and hyperventilation. Yet, I give this form of therapy two thumbs up, as I have slowly and gradually begun to forgive myself.

My therapist has been all over my head in the last few months, starting with my recent severe depressive episode to my blocking belief that I don't deserve to get better. While the latter is no more an issue, I have yet to return to everything that has happened a little over a year ago. As we have progressed in therapy, he and I have realized that my mental illness, particularly my postpartum, was the catalyst to the greatest episode of depression. We decided to dive into that time in my life.

I was asked, if I summed up my whole postpartum depression and anxiety episode, what one memory is the most painful. It wasn't too easy to choose. Those months were a time frame I would like to forget and one I thought I was emotionally over. I was not. Thinking back, the most painful memory was myself, sitting in the ER with my mother next to me, waiting to be seen.

It was the old ER, as my local hospital has recently been renovated. Low ceiling, beige walls. Office chairs with fabric, grey in color, and black plastic handrails. The room felt so small and was pure chaos. To the right of me were the check-in stations with the workers behind a half wall with glass above. To the left of me were more of these common office chairs filled with other people waiting to be seen. In front of me was a wall with a floral framed picture and the entrance to the ER was to the front left.

Although the other people in the room were talking and moving, I was slightly out of my body in my own pure hell that I was still unaware of. My main reason for going to the ER was the simple fact that I must be malnourished and dehydrated since everything that went in my body quickly came out. I was rocking back and forth, with my hands gripped so hard on the handrails they were in pain. In addition to this, I was shivering as if the temperature had dropped to zero degrees Fahrenheit. Hyperventilation was present, and tears streamed out of my eyes non-stop.

"When did this happen?" asked my therapist.

"Exactly a month after Sophia was born," I said.

"Let's go with that." he said.

That was my cue to close my eyes and allow the Thera-Tappers to do their work. Buzz in my left hand, buzz in my right, repeatedly. I started looking at Postpartum Stephanie, and as anxiety churned my stomach, I could feel tears well up. I wanted to hug her.

"What do you feel?" he asked.

"Sadness for her. She must have been scared. She has never been through this before."

"Been through..."

"The intense anxiety, the panic attack. This is new. All my bouts before were just depressive. This was my first where anxiety made an appearance."

"What do you think you needed back then? Someone to have done something? Said something?"

The first round of EMDR with this question stumped me. I had the support of my family. I was seeing a psychiatrist and a therapist. I was on medication. What did I need back then? What would've helped me? We tried again and instantly, it came to me:

"I needed someone who had been through this hell to tell me everything would be okay. I would've believed that person because they would have experienced what I had or something similar. All these other people telling me it would be okay didn't help. They didn't know what I was going through. The postpartum community was small back then, over nine years ago."

"Put yourself in the ER, yourself now. Think about it. What are you doing? What might you say to yourself now."

He turned the Thera-Tappers back on. I closed my eyes and returned to that scene. The present me was kneeling on the floor of the ER with my hands on the knees of the Postpartum me. I could still see her rocking back and forth. Truly scared for her because she had no idea what she was going through. My touch an instant connection to the feelings inside her head then. I tightened my squeeze and looked up at her face. She had a blank stare at the wall ahead as the rocking continued. I noticed the fear in my mother's eyes as she wondered what was going on with her child. I turned back to former self's face and I spoke:

"It will be alright. You will be okay. I know you will be okay because I've been there."

The second I said, "I've been there," Postpartum Me's eyes focused directly on mine and she stopped shaking. I kept repeating it over and over, "I know because I've been there."

It was the first time I showed my Postpartum Self some self-compassion.

Team Work
May 13, 2016

I NEVER HAD a psychiatrist I loved. Heck, I never had one I liked. Honestly, my relationships with my psychiatrists these last two decades don't even measure up to an "acquaintance" standard. They are short, sometimes snippy, and barely lift their eyes off their laptop to make eye contact. These are the doctors who control what medications I take, and I am only in their office for a whopping 10 minutes…

It bugged me yesterday as I sat in the waiting room for my appointment. I wasn't even meeting with my normal psychiatrist. I had a sub-psychiatrist for this visit as my normal doc was out on maternity leave. No big deal, it wasn't as if I were close with her, even after seeing her for over a year. I entered my sub's office where he asked me the typical psychiatrist questions:

"How are you feeling?"

"How are the medications working?"

Yada, yada, yada.

I thought maybe he at least read my file before meeting with him, but nope, he didn't. I had to tell my story of the last year to him as quickly as possible as I only had about two minutes left on the clock of my appointment. And like that, my 10 minutes were up. I am not sure what was accomplished, as this man knows nothing about me and just handed me prescriptions for controlled substances. Upon leaving,

I made my next appointment. I asked the receptionist who I should make it with and she responded, "It doesn't matter. Your regular doctor will be back then if you would like to see her." Then was three months away. Then was almost at the end of summer. Then was August.

On my drive home, I really thought about the mental healthcare system in the United States. I even crowdsourced to see if my revelations about the system had merit and wasn't shocked with the answers, but I should have been. Most of the people who responded to me agreed that they had appointments with their psychiatrists that lasted up to 30 minutes at most, but it was more like 10 minutes where only drugs were discussed. These people then revealed that like me, they saw a therapist weekly or biweekly for an hour or more at a time. And the kicker, these team members never conversed with each other about care!

This is what angers me. I've signed waivers to no end that enables my psychiatrist to contact my therapist (and vice-versa) concerning my care and they never have. There are waivers signed for them to contact my primary care physician (PCP)... never have. This situation was even more complicated when I was hospitalized. I had additional doctors, several hospitals psychiatrists, along with my therapist and regular psychiatrist and there was still no contact. Amazingly, the hospital psychiatrists didn't even converse with each other.

I thought some more. How can I receive the

best care possible when my "team" chose to be independent workers?! I became the go-between, the third-party mediator. This was all fine and dandy for now because I am doing well, but a couple of months ago when I had a breakdown… wouldn't it have made sense for this "team" to talk? It's bad enough as the patient that your medications are a trial and error affair, taking weeks or sometimes months to get correct, and now you, mentally impaired, need to be able to handle the negotiating between your "team?!" I understand from a work perspective, as I hold a full-time job myself, that it is hard to fit things in. Asking these psychiatrists to talk with their patients' therapists is another step to make in a busy job they already do. Think about it… if they work eight-hour days and see four patients an hour (although 15-minute appointments are a stretch), that's 32 patients a day.

Thirty-two patients a day… that's almost 200 patients a week! I'd be shocked if they knew my name without looking at their laptop when I came in! But they should. They are dispensing medications that can be harmful. These medications carry some serious side effects, some that even include suicidal thinking. With this knowledge, wouldn't it be a wise decision to discuss the patient's condition with both their PCP and their therapist? Get an idea of who their patient really is?! See if they have any medicinal allergies they are lying about? See if they are known to hide their suffering to an extreme?

How do we accomplish this? Among my

crowdsourcing was a therapist, and she agreed she would rather be doing the team method, but that it was hard to enforce. By not having our teams discuss our care, we are really at a disadvantage here in the United States with mental healthcare. We need this system to be audited, to be dissected, and to be resurrected in a way that really has the patient's care at the core of the system.

Sound Meditation: Am I in That 1 Percent?

May 27, 2016

I SEEM TO BE a star pupil when it comes to EMDR therapy, so much so that we have taken a break from it and returned to CBT. My therapist, after months of reprocessing certain devastating memories... T., losing him, losing myself, my postpartum fiasco... decided I needed to learn how to cope successfully.

Key word: successfully. After being on this earth for more than 36 years, I should learn how to "cope" with my tragedies, both big and small. Instead of stuffing them to some corner of my brain and locking them away, I need to face them head on. I need to embrace them. After years of CBT, you would think I would know by now how to "cope." I don't. It seems that with every episode, I start out as an infant and need to relearn everything once again. It is rather annoying and downright tedious.

So after dealing with the typical "replace negative thoughts with positive thoughts" exercise, my therapist who is big on mindfulness and meditation, suggested we try exercises employing this. Why not? I am game for anything, therapy-wise. We decided to focus on a guided meditation dealing with sound. Why sound you ask?

One example... this Saturday night, as my husband and I were in the basement watching TV, our neighbors decided to celebrate July 4th a bit early. It isn't even June 4th. Even though we were in a basement that deafens the sound a bit with its concrete and insulated walls, I sat scrunched up in a fetal position with my hands on my head scratching at my scalp. I started rocking back and forth, curses flying out of my mouth. It was not a pretty sight. This sound, like my neighbors' annoying diesel truck and dirt bike is something I can't control. I dislike things I can't control. I am an alpha after all.

I sat comfortably in the soft cushioned chair upholstered in a floral pattern. My arms draped over the arms of the chair, my feet were flat on the floor. My therapist proceeded to get up, telling me that for this sound meditation we would, in fact, need sound. He opened two of his office windows and returned to his seat. He began to read from a book which directed me to close my eyes. Simple task, done. Then it got more difficult.

"Focus on the sounds around you. Those near and those far. Those that are long, those that are short. Those that are loud, those that are quiet. Notice how they fade in and then fade out…"

As he spoke these words all I could think was: These damn cars. They are so loud. How am I supposed to learn how to tune them out?! Okay, Steph, focus on the birds. You like nature sounds. Ah, birds, tweet, tweet, tweet. Damn cars! Shit, a motorcycle!

I was then supposed to imagine the sounds passing by like clouds. They roll in, they roll out. Instead, my breaths got short and rapid, my lank hands were now gripping the ends of the arms of the chairs, my head felt like it was being squeezed. I was nauseous, dizzy, tense, and a few seconds away from getting up and shutting the windows myself. The sound was too much for me. I was having a full-blown anxiety attack.

When my therapist finished reading, he looked up at me and asked me how it was. Being a great faker of feelings, he didn't notice any of the affects my anxiety was having on me. Between rapid breaths I asked, "Does it get better?"

"Does what get better?" he replied.

"Meditation? I am having a freaking anxiety attack."

"Hmm… this exercise is supposed to have a calming effect," he responded.

"So was the Container Exercise. I seem to be in this 1 percent where meditation has the opposite effect," I joked, "My head feels like it is being squeezed in a vice."

At this point, my hands were in tense fists. I felt as if I would vomit soon. I just wanted to leave. I needed fresh air. I needed space. I needed….

"Would you like to try this again?" he asked.

My eyes widened in horror, "Like now?! I am still coming down from my attack!"

"No, not now. I can see how distressed you are right now. But could we try it again with the windows closed focusing on smaller sounds at another session? I think you should give it a try a few more times before ruling it out."

I pondered this. Obviously, this first time did

not yield the response he or I wanted. Neither did EMDR for at least the first month of doing it, but eventually, it worked wonders. I knew I needed to get over this sound annoyance thing or I would forever be enveloped in my anxiety. I trust my therapist and agreed to try it again. The battle continues.

Rebound Insomnia, Really?!
May 31, 2016

I ALWAYS FOUND it senseless and cruel that most antidepressants, at least the SSRIs, take more than a month to fully be functional. Is this a colossal joke?! What depressed person wants to hear, "Hey, you'll be feeling much better, just wait another month or two!" Having already suffered badly, sinking into further depths of not recognizing your brain, further days of losing sanity, you now must wait. Tick tock.

Slowly weeks one and two pass and your anxiety increases… "Why isn't this damn drug working?!"

Week three shows up and you question if anything is different… "Wait, was that smile for real, or was it still my masked cover-up?"

Week four comes and one day you wake up and you can tell you are different… "Hallelujah!!!"

Six times and I am still not quite used to this adjustment.

What the doctors don't tell you is what you may experience when you come off a drug. For a few months now, I have been weaning off Seroquel, an antipsychotic I was prescribed while hospitalized in January 2015 for both its help with psychosis and also because it works mighty well as a sleep aid. This drug has had so many "lovely" side effects… weight gain, bloat, constipation… that I couldn't wait until I could go off this stuff. Several months after starting this drug,

I was no longer in need of it for its antipsychotic properties but still relied heavily on it for sleep. Then it stopped working for that and I had to add Lunesta in the mix. So why, why was I still taking it?! I started out on 100mg and after a few weeks went down to 50mg all under the supervision of my psychiatrist. About a month later (over two weeks ago), I went down to 25mg, the lowest dosage. Then, starting with this Sunday night, I stopped taking it.

And then I started to not sleep!

For the last two nights, I have had what is called Rebound Insomnia – rebound insomnia is when you can't sleep after coming off of a sleep medication. Because your body has become used to having the drug in your system, it is waiting for it. When your body does not receive said drug, it can cause short-term insomnia.

Seriously?! This is just cruel now! Even with .5mg of Ativan and 2mg of Lunesta, I am still experiencing rebound insomnia. It is now taking me more than an hour to fall asleep and I am waking up at 4:30 in the morning.

What to do, what to do. Do I cave, give in, and take the Seroquel? Do I continue hoping there is only a day or two more of this? There is already a panic brewing inside of me. I know how bad not sleeping is for me. It is a huge trigger for my mental illness.

Searching on the web, because the internet doesn't lie and is only there to scare you, I have found several people who complain because their rebound insomnia is going on for three weeks… three weeks?!

Okay internet, you've officially scared me. I can't go three weeks with my current sleep pattern. I'll wind up back in the hospital with them pumping me with large quantities of Seroquel and be back to square one. I refuse to give in. I logically know this drug is doing nothing for me right now. Without it, my digestive system will start to function normally again and maybe this extra 10lbs I've been holding onto since the birth of Seroquel into my system will disappear.

So, ladies and gentlemen, because I do not fully trust the psychiatric system, I want to let you know that there is such a thing as "rebound insomnia" and it is as cruel as finding out in the beginning that you will have to suffer another one to two months before you will feel better from your depression (if the correct drug is picked). I implore you to ask your doctors about the drugs you are on, their interactions and their rebound effects. It is your body, you should know what you may be in for.

Rebound insomnia... really?!

I'm Surely Dying
June 21, 2016

IT TRULY AMAZES ME how in the matter of just a few days, my body and my brain, can completely double cross me…

A friend of mine recently posted online that we are less than 200 days away from Christmas. This had me thinking about Christmas 2014 and my immediate family that was four in count at the time. I remember waking Christmas morning in our house with two very happy kids, my daughter and my foster son. He was smiling, his dimples poking his cheeks, realizing this is a happy occasion but not knowing why. There was laughter and much confusion from him as he had no idea what to do with a wrapped present. My husband sat on the floor by T.'s gifts and unwrapped them with the glee a child would normally have. It was a Christmas morning that was full of smiles, laughs and love.

Just a few days later, this all changed.

I had been having major anxiety off and on since T. moved in with us at the end of October. None of my spells lasted past a week. This was a warning sign and I refused to listen to it. I ignored the heavy breathing, the annoyance of every sound within my home… these things that my brain was telling me, "SOS, we need help NOW!" I didn't want to believe my perfect family, my dream family, was causing me to drown. I tried to suppress the angry feelings I was having toward my children to keep my dream of mothering two kids alive. I continued to go to work and act as if nothing was bothering me, dreading going home at the end of the day. I told myself, "This too shall pass."

But it didn't.

On the morning of December 30th, I awoke for work not feeling normal. I was shaking. My chest felt tight and I was dry heaving. Once again, I ignored my body's warning signals and went to work. I sat in my cubicle hyperventilating. "Deep breaths, Stephanie," I told myself. I stared at my breakfast with disgust. I was so nauseas that the sight of my Cheerios churned my stomach. I became dizzy, pushing myself against the headrest of my office chair to hold me up. I cried as quietly as I could to not clue my co-workers about what was happening to me.

Then the tightness in my chest produced extreme heart palpitations. This only fed my anxiety more as I wondered whether a heart attack was going to follow. My hand quivered at my keyboard. My eyesight blurred with tears I was striving so hard to hold back. I was scared. I had never felt this way in my life before.

And then the moment passed.

I thought I was in the clear when about a half hour later all the symptoms I had just experienced came roaring back. My body was exhausted from fighting it the first time. Professionals say there are two types of reactions to anxiety... fight or flight. I am the former. I fought so hard, I was dumbfounded I didn't pass out from fatigue. Just like the first time, I succumbed to exhaustion.

This cycle repeated itself over and over that morning. My co-workers were still clueless. Most of them weren't there due to vacation days they needed to use. I hid my terror from those that were with a fake smile. It was 1pm at work, which was lunch time. I went down with my co-workers and sat in silence, which was uncommon for me. I forced myself to eat as much of my lunch as possible. As they chatted away about TV shows, I sat... my heart beating out of my chest, the nausea increasing, my breaths become short and rapid. Yet, I forced the smile on my face. I left the lunch table slightly early. Back at my cubicle, almost an hour later, the symptoms weren't subsiding. In fact, they were growing in strength. I thought, surely, I was going to pass out and die.

I called my husband. He told me to use my coping skills from therapy. They weren't working. I said I needed help. I needed to go to the hospital. He could not take me because he was home with our daughter and foster son. Next in line was my mother. I called her cell but could not reach her. I then tried my father. Success. He answered the phone and tried to talk me down from this attack. I informed him this was going on all day, off and on. He said he would come and take me to the ER as I was in no condition to drive myself. I sat waiting for his text that he was here. I informed a co-worker as to why I was leaving in general terms to inform my boss. My phone vibrated... my father was here.

By the time I reached his car, he could see I was not myself in any way. I was a shaking, hyperventilating shell of a person. On the way to the ER, he asked me more questions that took me minutes to respond due to my lack of breathing. I was shivering so much, it was as if I was standing out in frigid temperatures for a long period of time which for December was common, but I was dressed appropriately. I felt helpless as my father had to help walk me in because I would fall over. At the desk I had to give my name, date of birth, etc. to the person at the ER desk. This I did with labored breath. My father then helped me sit until we were called into a triage room. I sat down next to the nurse in the room. At this point, I was just waiting for the heart attack. My heart was outside my chest visually in my mind. The pounding drowned out my hearing. I was still shaking uncontrollably, and my breathing remained heavy.

Her questions were not easy to answer. Unfortunately, me being an adult, my father could not answer for me. Then she got up and hooked me up to the blood pressure machine... 164/95. Next came my temperature... inaccurate read because of my strenuous breathing. This was followed by my pulse and oxygen... again, inaccurate. Upon completion of these tests I was finally moved to a room in the ER.

The ER doctor came in, asked me several questions, some the same as the nurse in triage. He took a good look at me. I could see the look in his eyes. He knew the suffering I was going through. The words came out of his mouth, "You are having a major panic attack." The good news, I wasn't dying. The bad news, I felt like I was. I was given .5mg of Xanax. Within 15 minutes of taking the Xanax, my body was beginning to calm itself.

At this time, I phoned my husband. Our foster son's social worker was over for what should have been a happy occasion. He brought gifts for the family for the holidays. After hanging up the phone, I knew what was going to happen. My husband had to tell the social worker where I was and why. I knew that my foster son, a boy I loved just as much as my daughter, would probably be removed from our house. This stirred the anxiety in me more, but I was drugged and extremely exhausted; I couldn't fight anymore that day. I just laid in the bed in the ER and breathed what were the first normal breaths of the day...

It was only a few short days later that T. left our home. It was a decision that both my husband and I (with agreement from our and his social worker) made in the best interest for him, our daughter and myself. It was not an easy decision... as a couple of people expressed to me after he was gone saying I didn't care about T.'s needs, that I was being selfish. The fact is, I cared so much about him, I knew he needed a mother who was not becoming a poster child for mental illness. I think of him daily. I smile at the fact that we taught him how to love, how to eat, and how to speak in the two months he lived with us. He is truly an incredible little boy who I will always love and miss.

.

Why I am Going to Stop Body Shaming
July 1, 2016

FOR AS LONG as I can remember, the words "fat-free" were a part of my everyday vocabulary. I am not sure when the switch to fat free milk was made in my house, but I don't remember any other kind as a child. It was during my elementary school years when cookies became bad, cakes were evil, and chocolate was a swear word. All of these possessed huge amounts of calories. It didn't mean too much back then as a small child. I had frequent birthday parties that I went to where I had the "sinful" cake. But it was starting; the body shaming, and I was learning it like every female before, from their mother.

I watched her turn down sweets, make lighter meals with every fat-free ingredient possible and often went with her to Ideal Weight meetings. I even attended a few aerobic classes. This was back in the '80s when Richard Simmons promised you a great figure if you just, "Sweat to the oldies." People only looked at the words "fat-free" and "sugar-free," knew it wasn't going to taste as yummy, but would be a good, healthier version of the real thing. So many times I tried to convince myself that those Snackwell cookies really did taste like chocolate heaven. What the heck was I thinking?!

My body shaming started around my pre-teens, 11, 12 years old. I started to compare myself with my friends, and couldn't help but notice I was a little bit chubbier than they were. While a few of them were still in kids' sizes in junior high, I had hit adult sizes and weighed almost 100lbs in my small 4' 9" frame. I looked at my thighs when sitting and just noticed how much they spread out. I saw the blob of knee fat I inherited from my mother's side of the family. I critiqued every aspect of my body. I was ashamed. I started dieting in high school. Every summer I would follow Weight Watchers, nit-pick at what I was eating, tell myself to do more exercise… still nothing was good enough. My size in clothing just went up to about a women's eight and I was at my max height of 5' 1." Nothing that is really of a huge concern weight-wise, but my mind was already made up. I was fat. I would never get a boyfriend, never be popular, never succeed.

Of course, the media didn't help. Everywhere from magazines to TV shows, women were shown as toothpick skinny and still are. Even as the years passed, it seems we have become comfortable showing bigger men on shows, but the women seem to get skinnier. What kind of message is that?

So, I kept myself busy. Like I do now to keep my anxiety at bay, I do anything that prevents me from thinking. I volunteered for the high school paper, the writing anthology, theater, anything. Then I became sick the April of my senior year and dropped 10 pounds in a week due to a kidney infection that prevented me from keeping anything down. I thought it was the greatest thing to happen to me because I lost that weight. That was awesome in my teenaged/young adult mind.

Just when I thought I had this weight thing worked out, I went away to college and put on the freshman 15, but thankfully, lost it with Weight Watchers over the summer. This cycle repeated my sophomore year. Unfortunately, the losing part stopped with junior year. By the time I graduated, I was 30 pounds heavier than when I started college and was feeling like a big fat pig. I could've taught a class in Body Shaming 101. This weight stayed on me when I married my husband and was still there when I was told that I couldn't continue living with my current resting blood pressure of 150/90. I had to do something, especially since we wanted to start a family the following year.

My doctor put me on a blood pressure medication, but basically told me I had to cut out all salt and perform some type of exercise activity instead of dreaming about it in my head. Sure, sure, I can do that. Day one, I put my sneakers on, disgustingly stared at myself in the mirror and did a few minutes of Wii Fit. Thinking some sort of weight loss miracle occurred, I ran up to the bathroom and went to look at myself in the mirror again. Nope, no change. Why was I doing this?! I was never going to be happy with body. But I continued and worked my way up over the next few months to exercising several times a week for at least a half hour. I lost weight. I was thrilled!

Then I got pregnant with my daughter and was even more ecstatic until I hit that period in my pregnancy when I didn't quite look pregnant yet, I just looked fat. Great. Now sporting a size 12 in pants to accommodate my little jellybean, I had to keep telling myself that there was a baby growing inside and that I wasn't fat. A few weeks later, it was very apparent that I was indeed pregnant. Once my daughter was born, losing the weight became very simple, but not healthy. I developed postpartum illnesses and was vomiting. By the time she was a month old, I had lost about 30 of the 40 pounds I put on while pregnant. I also was being hospitalized. After 12 days there, I was now eating, and eating a lot, and gained back 15 of those pounds. A few months later, I started attending Weight Watcher's meetings with my mother. And the cycle continues.

I had a great few years when the stars were aligned, and my mental, emotional and physical well-being were an amazing trifecta of strength.

Then, my mental leg slipped and dragged my emotional leg down with it. I was hospitalized again for Major Depressive Disorder and Severe Generalized Anxiety Disorder in January 2015. I saw my body go from 104lbs from not being able to eat when I entered the hospital and gradually rise the months following. I had hit 130lbs, 15lbs more than I wanted to be because to me 115lbs was my ideal. The weight only added to my Depression. I was stagnant… no energy to do anything and eating too much. A year later, this past January, I started counting calories. Still nothing. I kept up with walking at lunch, did Pilates at work, tried some fitness classes… nothing. Feeling hopeless, I turned inward and started to blame the most logical source, the three medications I was on to keep me sane. All of them can cause weight gain.

What I didn't see was my daughter. I didn't notice her there when I would question my husband on how exactly he cooked dinner down to every ingredient and amount used as I entered in the calories. I didn't see her when we went out to eat and I ordered a salad, mentioning I wanted to lose weight. I didn't notice she was there and at the prime age to take in and absorb what I was saying. I had continued and passed this thinking down to her.

"Mommy, I'm fat!" she told me one day.

I stared at her quizzically, "Where? Where is there fat on your body?"

My daughter is tall and slender like her father. She then proceeded to point to her stomach and the inherited knee fat. What have I done?! I don't want her to grow up like me constantly looking for body approval and yet, it has already started. But I didn't wake up that first time. After brushing off the comment, I continued to track my calories, discuss my exercise, and turn away those sinful foods... still in front of her.

Then I weaned off one of my meds, the medication I thought for sure was causing the weight to stay on. Yet, the weight didn't come off. I became sad and only discussed my weight obsession further in front of Sophia until I read two articles concerning body dysmorphia.

I reread them both and thought a lot about them over the last few days especially when my daughter complained she was "fat" again. If I continued to shame myself, I was not only hurting myself, but affecting my daughter's way of thinking about her body. And why was I doing this? Because I was barely shy of my goal weight, my perfect weight of 115lbs?

I am still on two medications that cause weight gain that I am nowhere near ready to get off. These meds help me live a typical life. I am eating well, exercising when possible, basically doing everything I can do. I am still relatively skinny.

As I thought about all this, I thought about how I could execute the "No More Body Shaming" plan. I have been shaming myself for around 30 years. It would not be easy. I am happy to report that for the last couple of days, I have kept my mouth shut. I still log my calories, but am now doing it when she is not around. I am learning to accept my figure and its "flaws." It is a start that I hope will reverse some of the damage I did to my daughter and create an appreciation for the amazing thing my body truly is.

Yes, Sure, You Were Sick
July 15, 2016

I'VE HEARD THIS so many times. I am not coughing. I am not sneezing. I am not complaining of chills. I am not home 'sick' in the term that I have the flu and need to be in bed. I would not spread my illness if I came into work. I would not pass germs that would in turn get you 'sick.' But I am sick.

Although I am not hacking or vomiting on you, I am, in fact, ill. I am afflicted with ill health or disease. I like to call them hidden diseases. These mental illnesses, anxiety and depression (and at one-point PTSD and OCD). It shocks me that when a person calls out sick, it has to be seen as a 'real' ailment to be deemed a 'real' sick day and not 'playing hooky.' The matter is, when I use a sick day at work, I am sick, but it is my mental illness that is center stage.

The last time I took a sick day where I was what is considered sick to a typical person was January of 2014 when I acquired the flu. For days I was bedridden, sleeping, going through chills alternating with being too hot, running high fevers and completely depleted of all energy. You know what, those 'fake' sick days, my body wants to be bedridden. I am usually dizzy and nauseas and it is my brain that makes me feel this way, no bacteria or virus I can fault. My brain, an organ I will live with all my life… not bacteria that will take up residence for a week. How can you not call that sick?

Through the years, I have learned to mask first my depression because I have lived with it for such a long time, more than half my life. I have just recently perfected the fake smile and faux happy personality when it comes to my anxiety. This little devil has been present in my life for the last decade and I never know when it will go on a nice vacation and I never know when it will return. Little bugger! Recently, it has decided to become the dictator of my being. It took over me a week and a half ago, making my body rigid and me mute. That day was the start to me feeling, well, off. The work week following that incident, I spent most of my days hiding in my cubicle, not wanting to interact with anyone. Many times, I wished I could just go home and hide in my room. I wanted to be alone. If I did have interact with my coworkers, I was the smiling funny person I usually am. All I must do is put on that fake grin and all my inner turmoil is hidden. Viola! I look perfectly fine.

This past Sunday night, I slept awfully. Even pumped up on .5mg of Ativan and 2mg of Lunesta, my body would not fall asleep. After watching the premiere of *Return to Amish* because, well, I had nothing else to do, I decided to try and fall asleep again. It was 1am. Luckily, sleep came quick, but my body awoke at five in the morning. Insomnia was back. When I finally decided to wake up for the day and not continue a fit of tossing and turning in bed in hopes I would fall back asleep, it was 6:30am. I gave in. Brain, you won. With a rush of dizziness and nausea, I felt it best to call out sick.

Upon returning to the office the next day, some comments were thrown at me about being 'sick.'. Sometimes it gets to the point where I feel like the boy who cried wolf. I have all these physical symptoms, but I do not look sick. I am on day nine of going to bed with such pain in my neck and shoulders because they have been tensing all day. I am highly unmotivated to move and feel out of it. I don't quite feel depressed as I do not feel hopeless or worthless, but I do not feel like myself. Some negative thoughts are returning to me... thoughts where my husband and child deserve better. I am frequently apologizing to both for being so irritable all the time. "I don't want to be mean, I am so sorry." As I am saying this, I imagine my daughter sitting in therapy in her adult years talking of her mother who snapped at her with anger all the time. It's not what I want, but I can't control it. Anxiety has taken the reigns.

And then, with the comments and the demons I live with, I begin to wonder if I am imagining these symptoms... maybe I am not 'sick.' This feeling only fuels the craziness I live with... now I am debating with myself if what I feel, mentally and physically, is actually real? Am I just saying this stuff for attention? I mean, I am the youngest child. Youngest children usually crave attention, but that was never me. I also am known to complain a lot, but not about my health. I have a high pain tolerance and usually wait until the last minute to get help with any ailment. Still, is this all in my head? Do I just feel ignored and want to be heard?

And then I take a step back and breathe. Damn that stigma. Just when I think I have broken through its barrier, I am sucked back into the vortex. This stigma is the reason people do not believe me when I am sick. I can't fall victim to it again, it will only hurt me. This is the reason I share my story all the time. This is the reason I explain to people what it is like to suffer with a condition that plagues your brain and interferes with your logical thinking.

I am sick and some days the pressure builds up mentally, causing physical symptoms and I need to take a day off, just like when having a fever. I need to rest. Any person deserves that without sarcastic comment. You deserve to be trusted.

I Had a Son
August 4, 2016

WHEN I MET HIM, he was just over the age of two with an adjusted age of about 18 months. All I saw were his deep dark sienna eyes and his messy brown-black hair.

I had a son.

He was all mine from the first day I saw him, anxious to give him a hug as I heard him "read" a book.

I had a son.

Soon after he moved in, scared about this new life, he began not to eat or drink, and worried for him, I began not to eat.

I had a son.

I watched him slowly develop the curiosity a toddler is supposed to have.

I had a son.

With each new discovery he made, I grew more love for him and more worry.

I had a son.

In that fleeting time he was with us, we taught him how to eat, play, love. We taught him family.

I had a son.

And when I left him, I was severely broken, pieces all over the floor.

I had a son.

I loved him so much, I craved to keep my family together, as I slowly killed myself.

I had a son.

And after he left, and the negative comments came from a certain person, my guilt grew… I was told I didn't love him, I didn't care for him, I acted selfishly, I ruined everything.

I had a son.

And every morning, I wake up with his face in my mind, sad for him leaving, happy he was ours.

I had a son.

And I always think about him. There is never a day in my mind where his dimple-cheeked smile does not appear.

I had a son.

A little boy who looked so much like a certain baby picture of mine, he could've truly been birthed by me.

I had a son.

I have celebrated his past two birthdays with a candle-lit cupcake and later, tears.

I had a son.

Now he lives with another Mommy and Daddy. The hardest decision I've ever made, but the best for him.

I had a son.

Each day I yearn to see him, to hug him, to kiss him.

I had a son.

Often, almost two years later, I am still smelling the clothes he came with. Inhaling everything about him.

I had a son.

My T.

*****

I wrote this during a bad day recently. Crying, full of tears. Shame and blame for T. leaving weighed heavily on me.

When I wrote this, I wasn't sure whether it was a poem or just a normal piece of writing. I am still unsure.

How My Sleep Divorce has Kept My Marriage Strong

August 25, 2016

I DON'T SLEEP with my husband.

We have tried for a few years to survive in the same bed at night to no avail. We just can't make that part of our relationship work. We have what now seems to be termed a "sleep divorce." In fact, aside from separate beds, we have separate bedrooms. It works, it makes us work. From the beginning of our living-together-relationship, we have always had trouble sleeping in the same bed. He constantly suffers from restless leg syndrome and every suggestion his doctor has given him to 'cure' it hasn't worked. Nightly, I would be awoken to the whole bed shaking, thinking there was an earthquake occurring because earthquakes are just so prevalent in the Northeast, USA (note sarcasm). Nope, no earthquake, just my husband's leg. He must be dreaming about running a marathon again. Ugh, sleep did not come easily those years and when I don't sleep, my mental illnesses take hold very quickly.

I am not completely innocent either. Because of my work schedule, I could stay up later. Being years before the invention of Netflix and tablets, this usually involved binge watching *Frasier* and *Golden Girls* episodes on my portable DVD player. Problem was, I was in the bed with my husband and tended to fall asleep during episode two or three, but the sound kept him awake. I solved the sound issue by wearing headphones, but then the light kept him awake. In addition to my DVD habit, I am told I also snore a bit and chomp in my sleep, but since I have not been given proof of that, I find that hard to believe.

So, when we moved into our four-bedroom house eight years ago, the excitement came. I could have my own room again! I think I was more ecstatic at the time than my toddler child. I looked at the remaining two bedrooms and declared the bigger of the two belonging to me. It had two windows and a ceiling fan. Yes, I had my own space. I could snore - I mean sleep - in peace. On rare occasions, when guests visited, I would vacate my room and sadly enter my husband's room to sleep. Luckily, those nights were few and far between.

I know many will not see this as normal. Let's rewind to more than a decade ago. My husband (then fiancé) and I were sharing an apartment with friends. This was right after we graduated college. We had a queen-size bed and a whole mess of issues between his restless leg syndrome and the fact that I was the one who had to wake up early. Constantly, I vacated the bed to either sleep on the den floor or the living room floor. Our roommates did not like this and ultimately, I had to return to that bedroom I shared with my husband and sleep in the maybe 18" wide space between the bed and the dresser. I would argue with our roomies to just give me one space to sleep in that wouldn't inconvenience them. There was no give and only the following response:

"How are you two going to be married if you can't sleep in the same bed together?!"

Ah... interesting. This response struck me. What does sleeping in the same bed have to do with a happy marriage? Isn't a marriage based on love and friendship? Where in the marriage license is there a box that we must check that says, "Thou Shall Sleep in The Same Bed Every Night?" Where is there a vow we are forced to take in the wedding ceremony that promises we will always sleep in the same bed together? My husband and I didn't quite understand the necessity. We both grew up with parents who didn't. Most nights, my mother would leave their bedroom to sleep on the sofa because my father's snoring became too loud and obnoxious. Once we kids left the roost, my parents had their own bedrooms for a while. The same happened with my husband's parents. My in-laws still have their own rooms. And you know what... my parents have been happily married for more than 50 years! Yes, you read that right, half a century! My in-laws aren't that far behind them.

My husband I have been married now over a decade and we have been together almost 20 years. This 'sleep divorce' keeps us happy and sane. We can sleep more solid and more continuous alone. Because of the better sleep I get, my anxiety is lower, and my depression is kept away. And you know what, my mental health is more important than the stereotype of married couples sleeping in the same bed, right?!

A message to all those men and women out there, those married or about to be, it is OKAY to not sleep in the same bed as your spouse/fiancé/significant other every night. There is no authority that says you must. Remember the first season of *I Love Lucy* where Lucy and Ricky had separate beds. Remember the king and queens of long ago who had separate wings of their castles. It is okay. Both of your sleep is way more important than sharing a bed. Getting healthy sleep keeps you mentally and physically healthy. If your spouse/fiancé/significant other is keeping you from having healthy sleep, you can make a change in the sleeping arrangements. 'Sleep divorce' is more common than you think and is way cheaper and healthier than going through a regular divorce (so I'm told).

When You Know It's Time
September 28, 2016

IT FINALLY HAPPENED. It only took almost two years, but it finally happened. I am proud to announce...

...I have tapered off Ativan!!!

This little, almost microscopic pill was in control of my life. Sure, I owe it some credit for saving me from body shaking, hyperventilating, heart-palpating anxiety. But... it controlled me. From the first moment that Benzo entered my system in January of 2015 when I was last hospitalized, I knew what would happen. I knew I would succumb to this drug just like I have so many times before to its siblings: Valium, Xanax, and Klonopin. Drugs that force me to relax (which is very necessary at the time). Drugs that force me to sleep, forcing me to become 'normal.'

For the longest time, I hated being on medication. I despised the fact that a little pill was necessary in my life to retain some ounce of normalcy. Every time I tapered off a medication, I threw a little party in my head to not being controlled by a substance anymore. I longed for the day I wouldn't be on any medication. Although it did occur and lasted for four straight years, I once again became dependent on medication, and many of them, that January.

When I admitted myself to the hospital, besides telling the psychiatrist I was having thoughts of hurting myself and bordered on having suicidal ideations (which I was), I had to agree to put myself on whatever medication they gave me. I needed the help, so I desperately agreed. That night I started on 5mg of Lexapro, 100mg of Seroquel and .5mg of Ativan, the latter would be given to me 3 times daily. I'll fully admit, I was a complete mess and was in dire need of the aid of medication in addition to therapy. I welcomed these meds with open arms.

After suffering on and off for decades, I finally decided to let go of my irritation at being dependent on medications. I welcomed it inside my 'guest house' for tea. (Please read Rumi's poem '*The Guest House*').

Over these last almost two years, I tried multiple times to taper off the Seroquel and the Ativan (yes, with the aid of my Psychiatrist – NEVER taper off by yourself). I failed on these attempts. I realized I was not where I needed to be mentally, and although I cried when these attempts were unsuccessful, I pushed onward and took my meds. It was only about four months ago that I finally, successfully, tapered off the Seroquel!

The next item on my agenda was to tackle the Ativan. Although I was not on the prescribed dosage from the hospital anymore, I was still actively taking .5mg in the evening for sleep. With this last hospitalization (and the events that occurred a few months prior) my anxiety at night was excessive. I feared bed time. I internally fought going to my room because I knew my bed was a cause of extreme anxiety. My therapist didn't quite understand this anxiety. After many visits with him, we figured out that it pertained to noise. My brain assumed every loud noise, hell, every noise would keep me from sleeping and when Stephanie doesn't sleep, Stephanie goes off the deep end. We processed my anxiety over loud noises, and although I'm still highly irritated when I hear any noise in the evening, I was able to talk myself down from the ridiculous thoughts that I would never sleep again.

I was now ready. The time to taper off the Ativan was now.

I consulted with my psychiatrist the best way to do this. At this point, I was down to .25mg of Ativan at night (have you ever tried to cut that tiny .5mg pill in half?!). I have been through tapering before, but I wanted her best recommendation.

She honestly said to me, "I think you got this. You know exactly what to do."

I started with 2 more weeks at the .25mg. Then I proceeded to .25mg every other day for 2 weeks and then, last week, .25mg every 2 days. By the time I got to my last dosage (Saturday night), I just said screw this and didn't take it.

So here I am, Ativan free for almost a week now and I am doing just fine. My bed does not scare me. When noises pop up at night, I logically tell myself it will not last and that the ear plugs will block it out. I've talked myself out of my anxiety without forcing it. I am proud of myself.

With all that said, please do not skew my view on medication. It is a valuable aid in mental illness recovery. I only taper off meds when I know I do not need them anymore, when I know I can live typically without them. I am off the Seroquel because I am not having a psychotic episode and it was not helping me sleep anymore. And I am off the daily Ativan because I do not need it. I still filled a prescription for it because when I do have anxiety attacks, I will take it. I am still on my Lexapro because after battling depression on and off, and after the suggestion of a few doctors, I have decided that it is probably a good idea to remain on an antidepressant for the rest of my life. I am more than okay with this decision. One day, I hope to taper off my sleep aid, Trazodone, but for now, I am content and living 'normally' and that is what matters the most.

How Being Hospitalized Saved Me
October 7, 2016

I GREW UP with the stigma that you never wanted to be known as crazy. Keep it quiet. Don't ever speak about it. It can affect your grades, your career, your relationships. Hush-hush, on the down low. I obeyed these commands for fear that because I was a diagnosed depressed person, I would only be crazy. I would be known as a woman who talks to herself or becomes violent because, well, that is how mentally ill people have always been portrayed in the media.

I'll admit, I fell victim to those views. I would thank God every day that I was never hospitalized. I could live in silence with my depression and fane happiness by putting on a smile. Day in, day out, I plastered that smile on my face, hiding the inner turmoil beneath. And then it happened, the day I feared the most, the day I had to be hospitalized.

At the time of my first hospitalization, I was deep into severe postpartum depression and anxiety. Honestly, I was extremely delusional and vaguely alive. My days were filled with multiple crying spells, several trips to the bathroom to vomit, not eating, not sleeping and spewing forth lies I believed that I didn't love my daughter or my husband and they would be far better off without me. The week before entering the hospital, I was at my new psychiatrist three times and my new therapist twice. Five of those seven days I saw someone to help me and yet I was getting worse.

The final decision to go to the hospital was based solely on the fact that I thought I was extremely malnourished.

My mother brought me to the ER. I spent the next hour pacing the room or rocking back and forth in one of the waiting area chairs, all while shaking uncontrollably and hyperventilating. My mother was extremely worried about me, beyond your typical Jewish mother worrying. She feared that my life was in danger. No parent ever wants to get to that point. Her fear never crossed my mind once as my only concern was my malnourishment.

I wasn't deemed an emergency because I was not suicidal or having thoughts of harming myself or my child. I did, however, have extreme thoughts of running away, of removing myself from this situation, this situation where I didn't love my daughter and wanted nothing to do with her. When I was brought back into a triage room and questioned by a physician's assistant, I explained quickly that I was one month postpartum and then angled in on my not eating/vomiting for a couple of weeks situation. The only doctor who was brought in to see me was a psychiatrist. This is where I was officially diagnosed with severe postpartum depression and anxiety. Her next question to me was:

"Are you willing to admit yourself to the short-term psych ward?"

That is when I started to shake again. Tears rapidly fell down my cheeks. Psych ward? But that is for crazy people! Me? Crazy? Quick visions of strait jackets and padded rooms came into view. Fear that I would be drugged and left for eternity entered. I would never see anybody again. But this is what you wanted, Stephanie, you wanted to run away and eradicate yourself from this world. Then I looked at my mother and my husband and said, "Yes."

My initial day is a blur. I was so out of it, physically drained from all the crying, vomiting and shaking. I think I attempted to sleep through most of it. Of course, I was drugged, but at this point didn't care. I didn't care about my well-being at all anymore. I could've wasted away to nothing and I would've been cool with that.

But on the second day, I was pulled from my bed and brought to group therapy with the threat that I would have to go home if I didn't 'participate.' Therapy brought on stories from others who were 'obviously' sicker than I was, at least that is what I thought. I heard their struggles and their successes. I was given food and although it was very hard in the beginning, I started to eat and guess what? I didn't throw any of it up. I was given coping tools in art therapy by drawing, crafting and journaling. I was becoming more human. Within days, I anticipated visiting hours when my baby girl would come to see me, and I held her the whole time.

Being hospitalized saved my life. If I didn't admit myself, I am not sure where my delusional thoughts would've taken me. The hospital gave me the 'Me' time I so desperately needed. It gave me a break from my responsibilities to others and forced me to take care of myself first. It gave me medication that got me stable (although apathetic). I felt safe there, safe from myself.

I felt so safe there that when, eight years later, I needed help badly, I knew I needed to be hospitalized and begged for it. Once again, I was riddled with extreme anxiety that had me nauseas from sunrise to sunset. I had lost lots of weight and was grieving the loss of my foster son to child services. This time I was worried about myself. This time I had thoughts of hurting myself. This time I cared about getting better. I, not ashamed, admitted myself to the same short-term psych unit I was in all those years ago. I did it because it saved me then, and I knew it would save me now.

Being hospitalized wasn't perfect. The psychiatrists were basically non-existent during my visits. Both stays contained weekends and holidays, days that doctors didn't work. It's like us patients could put our issues on hold until they came back. The life-saving measures I found in the hospital happened through myself being able to focus on me, medication, their slipper socks (still feel safe in them), and its therapists and nurses. They were nice and didn't treat us as a threat to society. We were respected. We were people.

I don't hide the fact that I have been hospitalized. It is not a hush-hush situation for me anymore. People need to know what it is really like. People need to know that anyone around you; your parent, your coworker, a friend, could be battling a mental illness, and may be or have been hospitalized. People need to know that *One Flew Over the Cuckoo's Nest* is not typical.

A Depressive's Day of Feeling Depressed

January 4, 2017

EVERYONE HAS DAYS when they feel sad, hopeless, empty. A day here and there when nothing seems to be going right. A day where getting out of bed is a struggle you don't mind losing. The good news is most people, typical people, wake up the next morning and are ready to take on the world. They woke up on the "correct side of the bed." They can easily carry out their normal routines and enjoy things.

This, unfortunately, is not the case of a diagnosed depressive.

I've been unwell for so much of my life, that sometimes I am unsure if I am better, if I have overcome the latest episode with severe depression and her sister, severe anxiety. I can easily tell when I have clawed my way out from the quicksand, my head finally above the surface, but the last few inches seems like an eternity to rise from. Living with these two, even when well, is a constant battle and a huge drain on my battery.

I fear mornings when I wake up and know I'm off. I feel the melancholy taking over. My heart is a void, all emotion down its drains. I don't want to move. I want to remain in my bed. Soft, yet firm mattress. Warm blankets. A cozy cocoon. If I stay there, I will feel safe. I know though, that I can't. Years of therapy and battles have taught me I need to force myself out of bed.

So, I rise.

I walk slow, feeling the weight of my body all pushed down to my feet. It's an extreme struggle to take a step, but I push onward. Dragging myself to the kitchen, I carry out my routine starting with feeding the cat. After, I climb the steps, trying hard not to crawl up them and enter the bathroom. I plug my flat iron in and start it and brush my teeth. The routine is killing me on the inside. As I gaze at myself in the mirror, those horrible negative thoughts come back:

"Why get ready? Why go to work? They will be just fine without your worthless self."

"You look horrible."

"You don't deserve love. You don't deserve your husband, your daughter, your family, your friends."

I hold back tears, repeatedly telling myself that this is my inner bitch talking, not the real me, the real Stephanie, ultimately failing at convincing myself.

Somehow, I manage to get dressed and somewhat care about my appearance for work, hiding my inner dialogue and turmoil from those around me with the elusive faux smile. In my time, I have become an expert at it.

I get to work, still sporting the fake grin, but once in my cubicle, it is shed away. I become quiet, a recluse. I do not want to leave the cubicle. I do not want to interact with anyone for fear that they may see what is going on with me. I just desire to sit in my chair all day. On and off, I will fight back tears. Sometimes a few will make their way down my cheeks. I don't care if the sun is out, if the weather is beautiful - I want to stay hidden, be invisible.

When I get home, I am exhausted. Heart still empty. Body still drained. Mind still double-crossing me. I permanently erase the smile as I walk through the door. At this point, my 10-year-old daughter instantly notices and says to her father who is in the kitchen preparing dinner, "Mommy is having a depression day." Yes, baby, Mommy is.

Dinner is spent with me looking down. I play with my food. Some of it makes it into my mouth. I am not hungry. I just want to go into my room and hide. I have no desire to watch TV, read, play games on the Kindle. Even scrolling through my Facebook feed doesn't appeal to me. I just want to be alone, alone with my hopeless self. When I finally am, at the end of the day, tears fall… and every negative thought I have or action I've done feeds them.

I take a deep breath, swallow my pills, and eventually fall asleep hoping that tomorrow will be "normal."

A day that most people have occasionally, but I am not the typical person. Most times, I do not wake up the next morning feeling better. It can take me a week or more to wake up "normal." This frightens me. Experts say that after two or three weeks of feeling like this, that you are entering an episode of Major Depressive Disorder, that you are clinical. I am already clinical, so what is the big deal, right? I fear another episode with the severe sisters. My episodes have only gotten worse as I get older. This last one took just about 2 years to get through. What would the next episode do? Would I survive the seventh episode?

This happened to me recently in December. For over a week, 10 days, I woke up like this. Over a week, I didn't exercise. I didn't even take my daily walks at lunch that I typically love so much. I was getting worried. I saw my therapist during this time. Even he looked a little concerned. He assured me that I could contact him whenever, day or night, if I needed to.

Then on the morning of day 11, I woke up fine.

I've Always Wanted to be an Architect, and Other Shit

January 11, 2017

I REMEMBER my first Lego set. I was six and my family had just gotten back to my Aunt and Uncle's house from the mall. I am not sure why I wanted this set so badly, but I begged, I pleaded, and now it was lying on the floor of the bedroom I was sitting in. It was a medieval boat that came with two men in helmets. I stared at it in awe. Could I build this? At six?

I worked hard on it and sure enough, I completed it. I stared at it in amazement thinking, *Wow, I built this!*

This teeny-tiny itty-bitty Lego set started it all. I wanted to become an architect.

Through the years, I challenged myself. The sets got bigger and my time to build them got shorter. I would follow the directions, quickly erect the Lego building, look at it with pure elation and then take it apart. At this point, I would build my own creations. I was, after all, a budding architect!

As I became a teen, I shifted from Legos to hand drawings. I would draw floor plans just for fun. Soon, I developed into drawing the front elevations of houses. I received several home plan books and computer programs for my birthday and holidays. I even received a drafting table. Yes, this is what I wanted to do.

In the fall of 1998, I started the Bachelor of

Science in Architecture Degree at the University of
Maryland. I was on my way. For the next few years, I
lived in the architecture building, taking an interest in
my architectural history courses. I became fascinated
with buildings, mainly homes, from the Colonial and
Federal time periods. I graduated in May of 2002 and
after a month, started my career in architecture.

But I was far from my desire to be a licensed
architect. I kept my work records and when the time
came, I began to study for the exams; seven tests that
cost over $200 each. I took my first exam when my
daughter was a toddler. I anxiously waited for my
results. The day finally came...

...FAIL.

I was heartbroken. I was also amid my fifth
episode of depression. I decided to take a break and
wait for my daughter to get a bit older. After all, the
five year rolling clock didn't start until you passed one
of the exams.

1 year after I failed the first exam, I took a
different one. I felt confident going in. I felt happy
when I left. I felt defeated when the results came...

...FAIL.

The word 'fail' and the fact that I am an alpha
with perfectionist tendencies, didn't ease this
situation. I decided then and there, I was done taking
exams until I had the money to pay for the review
courses and the exams.

Years went by. My job growth continued,
although minimally. I began to really think about my
career. Would being licensed make a difference? At

that point, no. My pay would not increase. My responsibilities would not increase. Why spend the money? Just so I could put 'architect' after my name?

A few years ago, I was struggling with my career. Where I was working was affecting my mental health greatly. It was not a healthy place for me anymore. Once again, I thought about the question:

What do you want to be when you grow up?

Suddenly, the answer was no longer architect. I had become increasingly interested in hiking and nature. Being outside rejuvenates my soul. Researching, I realized that maybe a career in forestry, such as becoming a park ranger, would be for me. Lacking funds to go get a degree in it, I decided to start small and take a Certificate Course in Forest & Wildlife Conservation. Most of the material intrigued me. And then reality set in... there were very little, if any, paying positions in the Northeast and we were not moving.

Next up in line, a Groupon became available to become a Certified Personal Trainer. I studied and miraculously passed the exam (an exam that most of its material was not covered in the books the course came with). To this day, I am still certified and have not used it.

Why? I changed jobs. I found a job that still uses my knowledge in architecture that I enjoy. Is it my passion?

...No.

I feel like we stress deciding a career so early in life. Of course, I made the decision even earlier than necessary. I graduated college when I was 22, but one had to declare a major by the end of sophomore year. I look at my daughter now and can't even believe that in such a short amount of time, she will have to decide what she wants to do with the rest of her life. How can we decide so young with so little knowledge and experience in what life really is? She is already starting to decide. So far, she has narrowed it down to fashion designer, illustrator, and teacher (fashionista dropped off the list a couple of years ago). These are her current passions, but when she is my age (a few years shy of the big 4-0), will she still feel that way? I don't.

If I could turn back time (someone send me a Time Turner from *Harry Potter*), I would change my major, knowing what I would endure in the years to come. Becoming an architect would fade away. After suffering severely with mental illness, advocacy is my new passion. I only want to help others to not suffer the way I have and to get better. I want others to know they are not alone. I want to be one of the many people to break down the stigma wall, block by block. If money were not an issue, I would go back to school now. I would get a degree in Mental Health Counseling. I would become a counselor. Since money does not grow on trees, I will do what I can, maybe one day going back to school.

For now, I am an Architectural Project Manager who advocates for Mental Health and Maternal Mental Health through my writing. And, I am content this way.

When False Information on a Meme Makes You Angry

June 23, 2017

THE OTHER DAY on Facebook, I came across a meme. This shitty ad that basically told me and others who are mentally ill and medicated that we are now drug addicts. While addiction is part of mental health, I have not been diagnosed with it. I am a long time depressive and anxiety-ridden mom who will fully disclose any part of my history because people need to know what it is really like to be ill.

When I saw this, I was outraged, furious, and this was on a weekday morning in my cubicle at work:

"This is an antidepressant (image of a forest). This is a lifelong addiction (image of pills and pill bottles)."

What made this worse was this was the pinned post in this group 'The Free Thought Project.' My blood was boiling. I wanted to break something. Instead I decided to use this as an opportunity to educate.

I have seen many versions of this ad before telling people that medication is evil and while I find them offensive, it didn't hit me as hard as saying I now have a "lifelong addiction:"

This medication shit… well I will flat out admit I wish I didn't have to take it, but comparing it to the stuff that would be on my daughter's diaper years and years ago is a bit much.

Nature as an antidepressant... I agree wholeheartedly that nature is very rewarding. I am an avid outdoor enthusiast. I love being outside. After a hike, I usually find myself rejuvenated, feeling alive and most importantly, happy. A hike or a walk outside at lunch can 'turn my frown upside down.' There are just a couple of things wrong with this statement: Nature does not have the same effect on everyone and when you are severely depressed, it isn't going to work. Trust me, I've been there.

Being an alpha personality, a control freak, a perfectionist, I will fully admit that I hated being on meds. I couldn't fathom the idea that a little pill (or four) controlled me. I was only 'normal' because of them. I thought I could get better without them. I was wrong... very, very wrong.

The first time I was prescribed medication was shortly after my 18 birthday. It came in the form of a half white and half aqua capsule known as Prozac. I was quickly told not to tell anyone I was taking it. This was after I held a case cutter I stole from work to my wrist, debating whether I should live or die. This event, I was also told to not speak of. Because of this, I thought medication was wrong, bad, sinful. How stupid of me.

It wasn't until my recent episode almost three years ago that while getting better, I finally said, "Screw it!" I didn't care who knew. If I had a megaphone, I would probably be screaming it. There is nothing wrong with being medicated. I really should create (or order if it exists) a shirt that reads:

"Medicated & Proud of It."

These people who create these offensive and naïve memes have no idea what it is really like to live with these conditions. Because it is invisible, it doesn't exist. There is no official blood test or genetic test, we all must be making it up. It is all in our heads… why yes, it is. Because of a lack of serotonin, something produced in my brain (i.e. my head), I live daily with two severe illnesses. I am not making it up. Who would make up paying monthly for medications, weekly psychiatrist & therapy appointments, being hospitalized, becoming severely delusional, considering hurting or killing yourself?! Yes, I totally want all of this!

But we live in a society that believes mental health is not on the same level as physical health. It is okay if you take lifelong medications for illnesses such as diabetes and cancer and that is not seen as an addiction. Why is it okay for them but not for people like me? Why am I 'faking it?' I wonder if there was a real test that proved a mental illness diagnosis if these views would change.

I have weaned off medications a handful of times. It can happen. I lived several years med-free before I entered my sixth episode. Once on medication again, I took a hard look at my husband, my daughter, and my parents and told myself I didn't want to see them suffer anymore. I didn't want to suffer anymore. I decided then and there to never ever go off my antidepressant. Lexapro and I will remain the best of friends. I am not ashamed of my med. Without it, I would be in a very dark place or not here at all.

To 'The Free Thought Project,' research more on what is truth and what is fiction. I don't care if you lean liberal or conservative. The inflicted are a large population and by posting this, you are making us want to hide more. Because of this, many people will stay silent. Because of this, many people will not get the help they need. Because of this thinking, more deaths by suicide will occur. Remember that adage, "Stop and think before you speak?" It would have come in handy here.

To all my fellow people with mental illness, please do not hide. Do not believe a word of this absurdity. There is help. A walk in the woods can help, but it is not a cure. It will not help as much as therapy and medication.

What Happens When a Dream Turns Into a Nightmare

June 30, 2017

SUDDENLY, I WAS back there. That place, both a saving grace and a hell. I was walking down the hall. Bare concrete block walls. Gray, solemn, just like the people who dwelled inside. Doorways on both sides leading to rooms with aging waiting room furniture that was once comfortable but now forlorn like their occupants. I was one of them again. An empty void, emaciated, internally crying for help. Tempered glass and a counter to my left held those who treated us. Their faces ranged from a gentle smile to a stare as if asking, "What is this person doing? Am I safe?" Slowly, I walked toward the end of the hallway where a window was. Large, a glimpse to the outside world. If only it was not right across the street from a cemetery.

My eyes were welling up with tears.

Why was I back here? There was no reason to be. I have been doing well mentally and emotionally. If this was the case, why was I, without warning, plunged into the short-term psychiatric ward once again? I was dreaming and being triggered. Being both on the outside looking in and on the inside, dying to get out.

I have a love-hate relationship with the hospital's psych ward. When I was first there over 10 years ago, I wondered why I was there. I never thought

I was experiencing the same problems as the other residents at the time. I thought I was normal. *Ha, ha, good one Steph!* When I went back over two years ago, I begged for it. I knew being there would help me.

There are things I would rather forget about the hospital aside from the bare walls and gloomy atmosphere:

The bed checks every 15 minutes; even if I was deep asleep, like clockwork, I was awakened to a flashlight shining into the small glass panel in the door.

The psychiatrists… although there to help, none of them appeared like they cared to help you. I spent all of five minutes a week talking with them while their eyes looked elsewhere as if saying, "You're wasting my time."

The wake-up time and routine… it was a bit rough waking up at seven with all the medications I was given and then to go through the process of waiting in line to get weighed and our blood pressure taken.

Lack of outdoor time… depending on your mental and physical state that day, you may be allowed to go for a short walk circumnavigating the hospital building, viewing the nearby cemetery and emergency room.

But where there is bad, there is also good. As I mentioned, I knew I needed to be hospitalized again. For some reason, I felt safe there. I was only responsible for myself. I could focus on my much-needed self-care and work on getting better, even if it took a psychotic break to get me there. I knew I would get the medications necessary to sedate me, stop my brain from its incessant thinking... you're worthless, helpless, not worthy of love. These medications would also stop my hysterical, borderline delusional, thoughts... take that screw, just jam it in your head, who cares if it kills you?!

Although the psychiatrists were lacking in care, there were some nurses who were a pleasant gift. They would talk with you about your life, focusing in on your face, treating you like a human being. They remembered things you told them and asked you about it days later. They were concerned about your care. Sometimes they even sat and watched TV with us.

Aside from two very special nurses (one each hospitalization), I made connections with fellow residents. We talked about our experiences, gave each other advice, was there as a person who knew what it felt like. I still, from time to time, communicate with my last roommate.

And yet, this dream triggered me. I awoke with rapid breaths, scared, worried, panicked. What did it all mean and why was it affecting me so badly? I was somber and perplexed the whole day. Was this a prelude of another hospitalization to come? Because of my anxiety diagnosis, of course, here I am jumping to the worst conclusion instead of calmly thinking this through. And if it is a premonition, why am I so fearful? The hospital helped me.

I Will Not Hide Anymore:
A Letter to the Non-Believer
September 27, 2017

TO THE NON-BELIEVER,

If I passed you on the street, would you be able to identify that I am not 'normal?' Would you cringe and slither away from me? Would you see me as different, weak, an attention seeker?

For years, I stayed hidden because of people like you. Taught to fear my diagnoses. *Shh, don't tell anyone.* I believed it. I played into the stigma. I did it for protection against what you might say or do. I feared losing friends, family members, even career opportunities.

And then one day I said, "Fuck it!"

It just became too difficult to hide, too shameful, too guilty. And why should I feel that way? To hide from you and your posse? On this day, many years ago, I stood up proud and said, "I have a mental illness." I would hide no more.

And you laughed because to you, these illnesses did not exist - do not exist. To you I was weak, finding life's normal stressors too hard. To you I was seeking attention, because you thought I felt ignored. It never once crossed your mind to believe me because hey, you can't see these illnesses so why the heck would they be real?!

It didn't matter that there were other invisible

illnesses that you can't see, but believed were real. It didn't matter that I was someone you knew for decades. It didn't matter that a fifth of the population would be diagnosed with a mental illness. To you and your fellow Non-Believers, I was making it up. It was all in my head.

All in my head. Yes, in a way it is. My head contains my brain. Mental illnesses are disorders of the, what? Yes, the brain. The brain, the thing that controls everything in your body. It tells your heart to pump blood. It tells your stomach to digest food and make energy. How could we believe that it could turn against us?!

But it can.

It distorts my thinking, makes me believe I am a loser, unwanted, undeserving of anyone's love and kindness. It tells me my friends and family can't stand me anymore. And in some cases, it makes me ponder hurting myself or if life is even worth living anymore.

Do you know what that is like? To fully hate yourself, everything about you, everything you were taught at a young age made you the cool unique person you are? No, can't be real, right? And then more emotions creep in, more lies that depression makes me believe, the guilt and shame to any wrong doing I thought I did.

I can't wish these thoughts away. Oh, how my life would be so much easier if I could. I would gladly take one day of a horrible depressive funk if I was guaranteed I would wake up wonderful the next day. Stay positive, you say. One of many phrases that are far easier said than done. Then you throw out remarks such as grow up, man up, snap out of it. You call me selfish for thinking about self-harm and suicide because obviously, to your Non-Believer clan, I am only thinking of myself in this situation. You think I am blocking what others may think or feel if I inflicted harm on myself. The problem is, you have never been there, have never been in that position of just yearning to shut the racing thoughts and emotions from your brain, of wanting to not feel like an empty void.

Oh, and the lack of physical symptoms... I laugh. My anxiety causes so many. Where to begin? Shortness of breath, heart palpitations, extreme nausea, dizziness, insomnia. In extreme cases, full blown panic attacks that feel like I am dying from a heart attack, vomiting, constant muscle tension and hours of rocking back and forth. You tell me meditate, go for a walk and my favorite, hug your child. Not bad suggestions, but when I am tensed up in the fetal position, unable to speak, trying to scratch my hair out, these suggestions are not going to happen.

And then the hospitalizations. You wonder why our government needs to focus so much resources into facilities. You think my two brief stays were a waste of time and money. Yes, of course they were... I so wanted to almost bankrupt my family to pay for these stays. That was my desire, can't you tell?! My response to you now is we do not have enough resources for people like me. There are not enough inpatient and outpatient facilities. There is not enough coverage through insurance for psychiatrist visits, therapist visits and medication. And there isn't enough because of you Non-Believers and the stigma you place on my population.

You call me a millennial with the way I am "overreacting." Life is hard, you say. Stop being so weak, you say. Everything will not be handed to you on a silver platter, you say. It doesn't matter that I was clearly born on the tail end of Generation X or that my parents raised me to be a hard-working person. You laugh it off thinking somewhere in my childhood they fucked me up. You would be sadly mistaken. Except for a genetic link, my parents taught me to be respectful, loving and a go-getter. They always told me not to expect everything in my future career because we all are easily replaceable. They taught me that working hard got you to where you wanted to be. You know, all the same things your parents taught you.

And now, I am angry. So, so fucking angry. Angry that this is still an issue, that many people who are diagnosed still feel they must hide, that they would be weak or a freak if they went for help. I am angry that so many people have taken their lives thinking that was the only way out because of you Non-Believers. Just furious, even at myself, that I thought I had to stay silent.

But, I am silent no more. I will continue to advocate for my community and myself. I will tell my story. I will not let the stigma become me again. And, I will not wish you to experience the hell I have been though that might 'turn you.' The internal suffering and the suffering of your loved ones because they can't help is too much for anyone.

Sincerely,
Stephanie Paige, A Mental Illness Survivor &
Advocate

When You Learn How Important Self-Advocacy Is
October 24, 2017

IN THE LAST 20 years, off and on, with my frenemies, anxiety and depression, I have learned quite a bit about living a life with mental illness. My first 12 years were in secret, keeping my mouth shut on anything relating to the words "melancholy," "empty," "sad." I was told to hide, told that the stigma would ruin any chance of a career for me, would isolate me and make me feel even more lonely than I already did. I was ashamed that my differences made me plague-worthy. Who wants to be friends with a psycho?!

Eventually, I got fed up… or I should say, extremely deeply depressed. I couldn't hide it anymore. My postpartum brought on my first step in becoming free of this stigma. I had to admit my illnesses to someone aside from my family. I had to tell my boss. I had no idea what would happen, if I would be let go for some stupid made up reason to hide the real dismissal of me being crazy. I had no other option though, I was hospitalized and in turn could not do the work I took home to do during my maternity leave.

I then started to tell some friends and upon seeing their genuine compassionate reactions, I realized not everyone believed the stigma behind having a diagnosis. It was from this point, about a decade ago, when I decided to screw the stigma and advocate.

I dove right in, starting with maternal mental health. I immersed myself joining up with a non-profit I found on Facebook one day. I bonded with fellow mothers who experienced similar events. Some of them proudly declared their stories while others still felt the need to hide. It was an amazing feeling to not feel alone.

By doing this, I began to tell my story to anyone at any given moment. It didn't matter if they never inquired about my illnesses. I wanted to get my story out there. I wanted to be a voice, a voice that was heard when many others were still so afraid to speak up. This was my main form of advocacy. I told my stories and frankly, couldn't care less if someone responded negatively, which was very rare. I rose up to the challenge of becoming a symbol of someone who could be successful and who lived with mental illnesses.

These last few years, I began to learn about self-advocacy, the need to fight for my own care. This is not always easy to do, especially when your own care involves a brain imbalance and what I like to call "thinking imperfections." In the beginning, I even wondered who would trust me to create my own care plan; after all, that required someone with a healthy brain, not someone who was mentally unstable. Now I don't care. Majority of the time, I am in my right mind and can decide things for myself. But this was not always the case.

Three years ago, things changed. I quickly went from a stable human being to one having a psychotic break. There was no point in creating a self-advocacy plan at that time because the change was so rapid that I could barely recognize it. One moment I could coherently tell my husband I needed to go to the hospital's inpatient psychiatric unit, the next, I was in the fetal position scratching my head repeatedly crying for the rapid thoughts to leave me that it hurt too much. It frightened my husband, my parents and my daughter. More importantly, in my lucid moments, it scared the shit out of me.

It was after this last episode that I became extremely involved in self-advocacy. I needed to be. I knew how my body felt, what my brain was telling me, how the meds were working. When I needed a different type of therapy, I searched for the therapist. I worked together with my psychiatrist at the time in weaning off two of my medications. I made sure my doctors and my therapist were aware of each other. I began to practice mindfulness and really took notice at how my body felt. There were no secrets anymore, no hiding.

And now, once again, I am advocating for myself. In the last two years and nine months, I have been through four psychiatrists/APRNs at the same psychiatric group. They all left for some reason. The first, who saw me through my worst, left to have a baby and never came back. The second I saw once and then he retired. The third, who aided me in my weaning and worked with me on medication changes, left to become a head for an addiction facility. The last one that I saw once in July, just sent a letter explaining that she returned to work far too early when she had her first child and was now pregnant with her second. She decided to leave the end of December. I was due to see her in January.

What to do, what to do? As I am waiting for my next assignment, whether it be a psychiatrist or psychiatric APRN, I am researching my other options because, well, starting a fifth doctor in three years at the same practice is kind of annoying. With my track record, the next was bound to up and leave, too. There must be other psychiatric groups out there. Sad thing is, I am only down to seeing them twice a year, just for prescriptions. I know for emergency purposes, my primary care physician would write a script for me. Where the problem lies is with my anxiety. It has been worse these last couple of months and I foresee an additional medication being prescribed. As much as I like my PCP, I need someone who specializes in psychiatry.

Self-advocacy is a process that can be very time consuming and mentally and physically draining. When it comes down to it though, it needs to rank high in the self-care process. The only person who is going to care as much about your care and health, is you. What I have realized is that having a care plan is also a necessity. This can be used when you know you are not mentally stable. It is a list of things for your spouse, parents, or even a special friend to tell the doctors when you can't. It allows them to advocate for you the way you would want to advocate for yourself.

Teaching My Daughter to Rise Above the Stigma

January 11, 2018

MY DAUGHTER HAS SEEN ME. She has seen me throughout her 11 years of life. She has seen me lose touch with reality several times, seen me cry uncontrollably many times, seen me at a handful of appointments. She has even seen me become hospitalized. Throughout all of this, she has stood by my side, supporting me any way a preteen can. She will get me my medication and water when I have an anxiety attack. She will tell me she doesn't want any other Mommy when I say she deserves better. She fights the stigma for me to "infinity and beyond" (a *Toy Story* quote that defines how much we love each other).

But even with all that she does to help me, she falls victim to the stigma when it comes to herself.

My daughter, diagnosed with an anxiety disorder at six, feared anything medical. She catastrophized thoughts in her mind, constantly thinking that she could catch diseases just by breathing it in. While these medically induced anxieties faded through the years, she still tends to get overwhelmed and will have minor panic attacks over things that she can't control. She is easily frustrated. She cries. She's a worrier and a huge empath like myself.

There have been several occasions where school was a trigger. When she started elementary school, they placed my daughter in the Special Friends program at my request. It was a program dedicated to giving young children a place to relax for an hour and talk about their feelings. I loved this program. She aged out after second grade. At this point, we started therapy for her to learn coping skills for when anxiety attacks hit. This helped for a while and she was able to stop therapy for a year or two. Enter a few major life events, moving and entering middle school, and her anxieties came back full force. Insomnia set in. Panic attacks over homework became present and therapy sessions returned.

Through all of this, I have been her advocate. I do not want to see her suffer the way I have. There was a brief discussion last year with the school nurse about possibly getting her further help, such as a 504 report, within the school system. She had been sent home because she threw up. The nurse knew right away after seeing my daughter through the years that this was related to her GAD, but due to the rules, I had to pick my daughter up and keep her home for a day. The nurse said that if this was in her file, she could return to school the next day bypassing the required 24 hours. I thought heavily on this and suggested to my daughter that we get the school more involved. Her response:

"I don't want special treatment. There are kids that need it more."

I respected that answer since the school year was almost over and we were switching school systems. She started middle school and things were okay for a short period of time. Then I noticed her getting heavily overwhelmed, crying and panicking. I brought the subject of getting more help from the school with her again. She hesitated and replied:

"I don't want special treatment."

I explained to her that it wasn't special treatment. Her diagnosis, which is in her medical file at the school, would be more known so that if she did have further issues, she could receive the help she needed, whether it be visits to the school psychologist or extra time on a test. Then she started to tear up a bit and said, "No, I don't want it. The kids will make fun of me and my friends won't like me anymore."

Oh boy. Because I have been fighting it so long, the huge advocate in me came out and I may have reacted a tad too intimidating for an 11-year-old. I was angry. I thought the world has become slightly better with mental illness, but I was wrong. I spoke, with a seething rage inside my head, sternly to my daughter:

"Do not feel that way at all. Do not, for one second, be ashamed of your diagnosis. So, you have an anxiety disorder. You have no idea what other kids at your school may have. Most likely a few of your friends have one, too. All that, all that you just said, that is the stigma talking. You do not have to hide like I did."

She began to cry a little. She knew I was right, especially after being such a support and advocate for me. She nodded, apologized, and went upstairs. I didn't know if it really sunk in, the words I said, until one afternoon she came home from school and was excited to show me a video she was working on in school in one of her classes. I sat and watched the video and was so enamored and proud of this child. Here she stood, in the crowded hallways of her school, talking about her anxiety. She didn't care if anyone heard her. She spoke confidently about coping skills and therapy. My daughter isn't hiding anymore. She's kicking the stigma to the curb just like her mom.

Blaming Myself for My Daughter's Diagnosis
March 12, 2018

I TRIED TO hold my tears back as I stared into my daughter's oceanic blue eyes. I could feel them welling up, feel the moisture increasing.

Not here, not now, not in public, Stephanie.

The dam was about to break. A tear or two escaped. My daughter was concerned and relayed this to her father on the phone. She handed my cellphone back to me and my husband proceeded to ask, "Are you okay?" No, no I wasn't okay, but do I tell him that? The silence was broken as he asked again. I told him the truth because even if I lied and told him I was okay, he knew I wasn't.

"I am about to cry," I uttered quietly so the other patrons could not hear me. My daughter and I were waiting for our dinner order to be ready at our favorite sandwich shop in town. It was last Friday evening, the start of the weekend, and my husband's Friday to geek out and play Magic. He wanted to stay home with me. I told him no, I didn't want him to blame me for not being able to play (even though he wouldn't, it was all in my head). I told him this knowing full well that I wanted his support, but feeling I didn't deserve it.

Our food order was ready, and we went home passing my husband's car on the way. When we pulled into the garage, my tears flowed like a high-pressure hose. My daughter wanted to know what was wrong although she could somewhat guess as she has been a witness to me, her mother, for the last 11 years.

"It's my fault, it's all my fault." My lamentation increasing as these words escaped my mouth.

"What is your fault, Mommy?"

"That you are the way you are. It is my fault."

This year has been extremely hard on her and because of it, hard on me. She has been in therapy since the fall and because of some reactions she has had during her anxiety attacks the past month, it has recently been suggested that she get evaluated by a psychiatrist.

When the recommendation was first made to me by her therapist, I have to say I was a bit shocked. I guess I never thought that her anxiety warranted a psychiatric evaluation. After a few hours, I must admit the stigma against mental illness set in; her seeing a psychiatrist would really mark her as someone who is mentally ill. I hurt for her. My husband and I discussed the evaluation with her. She has learned about the stigma, has learned to stand up to it (from her mom, of course). But even this, having the word "psychiatrist" associated with her name, caused her to want to hide. She instantly thought she would be medicated. Eventually, she became okay with the evaluation that is set to be done in another week and a half.

All this got to me. It pulled at my heart and ate away at it. The biggest fear I had when becoming a parent is that I would pass on my illness to her and I have. Her being in therapy never bothered me. I am a firm believer that most people would benefit from therapy regardless of a mental illness diagnosis. It was the mention of "psychiatrist." To me, like my daughter, I associate "psychiatrist" with "medication." Throw in the word "evaluation" and I was losing it. I held back my emotions for the sake of my daughter, but I knew eventually they would become very visible.

I spoke with my therapist about it. He told me it wasn't my fault.

I said, "How? How is it not my fault?! She suffers the way I do. I never wanted her to and now she is. It's only going to get worse."

He logically said that this is something I did not give her on purpose. There was no way of knowing whether she would be mentally ill or not.

"But I gave it to her. It is my genetics that did this. She is becoming me."

No matter how many people tell me it is not my fault (heck, even my intelligent daughter tells me), I still cannot stop blaming myself. I can't kick this feeling. She is already experiencing more than I ever did at her age. I mean, I wasn't even diagnosed yet at her age and here she is at 11 with five years of diagnosed anxiety under her belt. Maybe I am transferring myself onto her to an extent, already predicting the suffering in her future getting worse and worse as she ages like it has for me. No parent wants to see their child endure pain and illness. In this case, I didn't want her to endure the thoughts that I have felt, the fear I have felt, the hopelessness that I have felt. I didn't want her holding a case cutter to her wrist. I didn't want her desiring to stick something in her brain to end the constant negative thinking.

And yet it is beginning. The fear is already inside of her. And it was all my fault. How could I not feel blame? More importantly, how can I stop feeling blame?

Living with Someone Who is Mentally Ill:
An Interview with My Husband
May 11, 2018

I WAS APPROACHED by a friend who offered up the suggestion of doing an interview series with family members on their thoughts and feelings concerning my mental illnesses. I must admit, I had been toying with this idea for a long time and at this request, felt it was the time to actually commit to the series.

As much as we (those of us diagnosed) feel and think about when we are deep in the depths of mental illness, what do those close to us feel? Do they feel as hopeless? Do they feel frustrated with us? Are they so angry they are wondering why they are with us?

I interviewed my husband this past weekend. This is a man who has been with me since we were teenagers. He has witnessed most of my episodes. He has been through my hospitalizations, my self-loathing, my hysterical thoughts. And he stays. A lot of what I asked him, I knew the answers to (I mean, hey, we've been together for over two decades), but he did shock me with a few.

I present below my interview with my loving husband, Jimmy.

The Interview

S. Paige: What were your 1st thoughts and feelings

after witnessing my episode of MDD in college where I slammed doors and pushed you out?

Jimmy: I felt I had done something wrong to make you feel, like, the way you were feeling.

S. Paige: Were you angry? Were you upset?

Jimmy: Defeated.

S. Paige: What made you call my parents then?

Jimmy: I don't remember doing that. (He did, in fact, call my parents and filled them in on what was going on with me. I received a phone call from my therapist that evening and then the campus psychologist the next day.)

Postpartum Depression & Anxiety

S. Paige: Okay, let's go to something more recent. What did you think and feel when you got the phone call that I was at the hospital after Sophia was born?

Jimmy: … I don't know. I didn't know what to think or feel. I didn't feel.

S. Paige: Were you worried? Were you wondering what the heck was wrong?

Jimmy: No. I just thought that is what happened (after childbirth). You had a hormone crash. You had 'baby blues.' I didn't realize you weren't sleeping well. I didn't realize it was a thing.

S. Paige: Did you realize I was vomiting all the time?

Jimmy: No, I knew you were taking Ensure.

S. Paige: Were you and I living in the same house at that time?! You went to therapy with me. You went to the psychiatrist with me. You weren't concerned at all?

Jimmy: I don't recall going to the therapist.

S. Paige: This is proving to be a valuable interview (sarcasm).

Jimmy: I blocked these bad memories out.

S. Paige: How were those 12 days when I was in short-term psych?

Jimmy: Nonstop. I didn't have time for, like, myself. I was always visiting you or taking care of Sophia or with your parents or at work. I had no time for me.

S. Paige: Did that strain you?

Jimmy: I'll never eat at a KFC ever again.

S. Paige: (Perplexed) Why? What does KFC have to do with this?

Jimmy: Because that is where I would eat from the train station on the way to the hospital. And I just can't eat at a KFC ever again because I link the two together.

S. Paige: So, it is a trigger?

Jimmy: Yes.

S. Paige: How were you able to continue with that schedule?

Jimmy: Because I knew it would end eventually. There was light at the end of the tunnel. I know you didn't see the light, but I could.

S. Paige: I feel guilty for that (putting him in this position). Do you know that?

Jimmy: It's what I am here for. I'm the husband.

My 2nd Hospitalization / A Next Time

S. Paige: How did you feel when I went back to the hospital?

Jimmy: I had gotten used to it. It's just, like, a part of you. Every decade or so, you're going to have to spend a couple of weeks in the hospital. I don't know. I've just accepted it.

S. Paige: Are you okay with that?

Jimmy: Okay-ish. I would rather you not have to do that. But, it is part of who you are. That every time some major event occurs in your life and for whatever reason you can't adjust to the change, it is always a possibility that you could end up in the hospital for a week or two.

S. Paige: Do you worry about a next time?

Jimmy: No.

S. Paige: Do you think there will be a next time?

Jimmy: Probably.

S. Paige: Do you ever fear I won't recover?

Jimmy: Depends on your definition of recover. So, like, hopped up on mega-doses of anti-psychotics for your life type never recover?

S. Paige: Yes.

Jimmy: Yeah, that's a concern.

S. Paige: What would you do?

Jimmy: I don't know. I don't want to think about it.

S. Paige: Do you fear I will take my own life?

Jimmy: No.

S. Paige: How are you so sure?

Jimmy: I… don't know. I'm not so sure, but I am pretty sure.

Stigma

S. Paige: How did you feel about having your wife in the psych ward? Did that seem normal to you? Seem weird? Did stigma play into it?

Jimmy: No. Because… it's… it's… maybe for the people of the older generation than us. I might not tell them directly that my wife is a 'nut job' and she's spent time in the psych ward, but people our generation and younger are much more accepting of medication and therapy and needing inpatient stuff, but I might not be as open to the older generation.

Our Daughter, Sophia

S. Paige: As a parent, do you worry that she'll be like me?

Jimmy: I worry she is going to be like me.

S. Paige: Why, what's wrong with you?

Jimmy: I'm an antisocial, geeky, anxiety-riddled 'nutto.'

S. Paige: You do not have a disorder. You have

moments of anxiety. She has one already. With teenage years and hormones, do you worry she'll follow in my footsteps?

Jimmy: No, you're still alive and you're 38. She'll make it through. It's part of who you are, it is part of who she is. I wouldn't want to change either of you two.

S. Paige: Do you think because of what I went through, we're better equipped to deal with Sophia if she does fall victim to depression? I know we have done better dealing with her anxiety.

Jimmy: I just hope we're not biased.

S. Paige: That concerns me.

Jimmy: I mean, you're super biased towards never going on medication.
(FYI, I am medicated and fine with it)

S. Paige: It's not that I'm biased, it's just...

Jimmy: ... like it's a sign you're headed down that slope.

S. Paige: Yeah.

Jimmy: And I'm just like yeah, whatever, if it makes the slope less steep, then who cares?!

Changing Me

S. Paige: Did you ever just want to 'slap' the anxiety and depression out of me?

Jimmy: No.

S. Paige: Do you wish I didn't have either one?

Jimmy: Interesting   question. It's   hard   to answer. Because it's part of you and I love you. But would not having it make you better or different?

S. Paige: How do you feel overall with this (pointing to self)?

Jimmy: It's interesting. What's the point of living life if it isn't interesting?!

S. Paige: Why do you stay? Times I've said go, leave me, take Sophia. I'm a disaster, you deserve more.

Jimmy: I need you.

And lastly...

S. Paige: What would you say to a husband/father who was going through this with his wife or child for the first time?

Jimmy: Persevere, because there is light at the end of the tunnel and it isn't an oncoming train. It is really the end of the tunnel. It will get better.

Living with Someone Who is Mentally Ill:
An Interview with My Daughter
May 21, 2018

MY DAUGHTER has seen it all. From her cherub baby face to now, almost 12 years later. She is a remarkable child who has not only witnessed her mother's hysterics, but also her own with an anxiety diagnosis. My daughter, given the name Sophia Faye at birth, is the epitome of the meaning… "Wise Fairy." Sophia is an old soul and understands so much for such a young person. Many words can be used to describe her but at the top of the list are compassionate, empathetic, caring and loving. There are days I may miss her little toddling body and cheeky grins, but I love watching her blossom into the amazing young lady she is today.

When I decided to do this interview series, I knew I had to interview her. I have not hidden much from her. In fact, three years ago, I was so foregone that I couldn't. She learned about suicide at the tender age of eight and questioned me often about it. She knows I grew to hate her as a newborn. I've always explained things to her in an age-appropriate manner and often worried about her reactions, but she has always listened, digested and never ever judged. I am amazed by her and couldn't have asked for a better child.

<u>Sophia's Interview</u>

Me: How did you feel when I told you I grew to hate you when you were a baby?

Sophia: Fine.

Me: How come you were okay with it?

Sophia: Because I knew you didn't mean it.

Concerning three years ago

Me: What did you feel and think when I left the house three years ago to stay with Bubbe and Grandpa (my parents) because T. (former foster son) was triggering me?

Sophia: I don't remember that.

Me: I left the house because I couldn't stay there.

Sophia: But wasn't I there too?

Me: I don't think you came the first night.

Sophia: Oh. I don't remember. I'm getting old!

Me: (After rolling my eyes at that last statement): How did you feel when I admitted myself into the hospital?

Sophia: Scared.

Me: Did you know why I was there?

Sophia: No, I'm not sure. No.

Me: What did you think when you couldn't visit me in the hospital and had to stay in the cafeteria with Grandpa?

Sophia: I wasn't happy about it. I mean, I wanted to see you.

Me: Were you scared when I was released from the hospital?

Sophia: No, because I was happy you were going to leave and come home.

Me: You've been protecting me since the hospital stay. How come?

Sophia: Because I don't want you to go back to the hospital.

GAD, PPD, Depression, & Suicide

Me: Do you blame me for your Generalized Anxiety Disorder? And it is okay if you do.

Sophia: No.

Me: Do you blame anyone for it?

Sophia: No. Why would I?

Me: Do you wish you were 'normal?'

Sophia: Sometimes.

Me: Do you fear you'll have Postpartum Depression and Anxiety because I had it?

Sophia: Sometimes.

Me: Do you worry or fear you'll have a Depressive Disorder because I have one?

Sophia: I don't usually think about it. I guess, but that is only when I think about it.

Me: Do you know when I was first diagnosed (with Depression)?

Sophia: You were 14.

Me: And how old are you?

Sophia: I am 11.

Me: So, you are close to that age.

Sophia: Yeah.

Me: That's why I watch you a lot.

Sophia: That's not creepy.

Me: Not in that sense, Sophia. I'm not stalking you... Are you worried I will commit suicide?

Sophia: Very much.

Me: How come?

Sophia: You told me how you took a case cutter and almost cut your hand off (almost slit my wrist).

Me: I was 18 then.

Sophia: So?

Me: That was 20 years ago.

Sophia: You also said that if you go off medicine you're probably going to want to commit suicide the next time you have an episode (of major depressive disorder).

Me: Are you worried I will hurt myself?

Sophia: Yeah.

Me: Do you think there will be a next time?

Sophia: Yes, just because of events that can happen in the future.

Me: Like what?

Sophia: Like Bubbe and Grandpa dying or like the kitties dying and stuff.

Me: Do you think because of what I have been through that I am too overprotective with you about mental illness?

Sophia: Sometimes. There is no reason you should be.

Me: Do you understand why I am?

Sophia: Yeah. Because you don't want me to get

depression and stuff.

Advocacy

Me: Do you understand why I advocate for this?

Sophia: What does that mean, advocate?

Me: Why I share my story. Why I try to teach others.

Sophia: Yes.

Me: Do you see yourself doing that?

Sophia: I don't know.

Thoughts on Me, Her Mom

Me: Do you think I am a bad mother?

Sophia: No. Not at all. Why would I think you were?

Me: Do you ever wish you had a mother who wasn't like this?

Sophia: No.

Me: How do you characterize your mother?

Sophia: Worried, anxious, fun, caring, loving, sometimes depressed.

Me: Do you always relate mental illness stuff to your mom?

Sophia: Like different things other than postpartum?

Me: Well, I have had depression since I was 14. There have been others thrown in there.

Sophia: When I think of depression, I don't think of

you as, 'Oh, she's depressed,' I think 'she is still alive, and she is strong.'

Me: You see me as strong and a fighter?

Sophia: Yeah.

Me: What traits do you hope you get from me or do you see you already have gotten?

Sophia: I want to get your determination and your strength and sometimes your empathy because a lot of times empathy is good, and I want your mental strength.

Me: Any last comments on me, your mother?

Sophia: I love her.

Me: How much do you love me?

Sophia: To infinity and beyond!

I am truly grateful for this kid!

Thank You!

June 11, 2018

CALL IT PART OF a depressive's "12-Step" Program, but I feel the need to say thank you to the people in my life who have contributed to my better health and wellness. Considering the decades that I've struggled, this list can become rather lengthy, but I will narrow it down to my latest and greatest (note sarcasm) episode of major depressive disorder. Some people listed may shock you, but all have helped in bringing the strength trifecta back to me. I now feel strong.

Thank You To:

My Parents: You have never given up on me. Although we all struggled to understand exactly what was going on with me in my teenage years, you never pushed my thoughts and feelings aside. You never told me to "suck it up." You never told me to "just get over it." From the beginning, you both have sought out ways to get me help, starting with group therapy to Cognitive Behaviour Therapy and even medication. You helped when I was a few states away in college. You both have cried with me, constantly worried about me, but never ever left my side. I am extremely thankful to have you two as parents as many others do not have such caring and understanding parents in their lives.

My Husband: Oh, what we have been through… first

and foremost, thank you for never taking me up on my offer to leave me. I must have told you dozens of times to go, take Sophia and run. But you didn't. You stayed and took our wedding vows seriously. You loved me when I was "crazy." You sacrificed so much when I was hospitalized. You never gave up on me. Although now you are unsure of what to say or do when my illnesses make themselves present, I know you care. As Bon Jovi said, "Thank you for loving me."

My Sophia, my baby girl: How did I get so lucky?! You are the light in my darkness. So compassionate, kind and empathetic. You have never made me feel guilty or unloved by you. You worry about me to extents you shouldn't, but I appreciate it. You are always there for a big hug. Thank you for being you.

My Therapist: Hmm… I don't think I would be here without you. I came to you in the darkest moments of my life. Lost and completely hopeless that I would ever recover this time. CBT therapy wasn't working this time. I needed something more. It was fate that all I did was Google EMDR Therapists and narrow it down to who was more convenient in location. It just so happens that the most convenient turned out to be my saving grace. I had huge doubts that EMDR would work. Highly emotionally draining in the beginning, you helped me to reprocess the loss of T. and in turn, the loss of Sophia's infancy, my postpartum, loss of more children and even the loss of my former self. Thank you!

My Friends: From visiting me in the hospital to checking in on me through social media and texts, I am grateful for each and every one of you.

My Gym: Again, another choice of convenience to work and home, the gym has been a wonderful addition to helping me get strength in all areas of life. Aside from building up my physical strength (I can barbell squat 135lbs currently!), all the trainers, instructors and the owner have made me feel welcome, like I belong. I am not just a number lost among many. It is a close-knit family that I am thankful to be a part of. Thank you!

My Medications: Although the stubborn weight gain and selective side effects are an annoying pain in my ass, I am completely grateful that they exist. I used to hate taking these tiny pills to feel 'normal' but now I am thankful they help me to feel like myself. We have a strong bond that will never be broken.

And lastly…

Myself: I think this was the hardest person to thank. I spent years hating myself, years internally abusing myself. I didn't matter. I didn't deserve love. At points in my life, I thought I didn't deserve to live. I have come a long way. Battling depression and anxiety both physically and mentally, sometimes draining myself into complete despair… I've finally learned acceptance and because of this have become kinder to all aspects of myself. I am now happier and understand I cannot change the past. I am starting to live in the present, enjoying the little things in life… my daughter's smile, a chirping bird, pretty flowers. I want to live. I want to see what the future brings. Thank you, Stephanie, for learning to live. You are truly an amazing strong being!

About the Author

Stephanie Paige is a thirtysomething who has struggled with Persistent Depressive Disorder and Major Depressive Disorder since age 14, and Generalized Anxiety Disorder since age 34, with Postpartum Depression, Postpartum Anxiety and PTSD mixed in there. She is the mother of one beautiful daughter.

With the strength of her husband, parents, and her child (and 2 crazy felines), she has survived six bouts of Major Depression and has become a huge advocate of mental illness. She advocates through words on her blog, spaigewrites.com, Stigma Fighters and The Mighty. She is a contributing author to *A Dark Secret: Real Women Share Their Trials and Triumphs of Their Battle with Maternal Mental Health Illness* and *Stigma Fighters Anthology, Vol. II, Vol. III &Vol. IV.*

She wants to let others know they are not alone and that is her striving force to sharing her story.

CPSIA information can be obtained
at www.ICGtesting.com
Printed in the USA
LVHW080300260219
608768LV00017B/229/P